WINNING WITH FRANK CHAPOT

Winning
with
Frank Chapot

FRANK CHAPOT
with ARLENE J. NEWMAN

Breakthrough
PUBLICATIONS, INC.

For information address:
Breakthrough Publications, Inc.
Ossining, New York 10562

Designed by Jacques Chazaud

Printed in United States of America.

ISBN: 0-914327-45-3

Library of Congress Catalog Card Number: 92-082783

Contents

Foreword

by GREG BEST

*A*t this point, my start with Frank Chapot seems almost comical. After months of almost relentless pursuit by my mother, the venerable Frank Chapot gives in because he figures it's easier to give me a lesson than to continue to say no to her. What happened in that initial lesson and in every lesson since, both on horseback and off, is what Frank tries to cover in his book.

Originally, when I heard Frank was going to write this book, I chuckled to myself. Anyone who knows Frank knows that he is a man of very few words, very few. So I waited to see if it was really going to happen. Maybe it would end up being a picture book. Well here it is, complete with words and pictures. But before you gain the benefit of Frank's knowledge, I get to share a few of my experiences with you.

Before taking lessons from Frank, I had other instructors and showed in the hunter and equitation divisions. But Frank was like no other instructor I ever had. When, at the age of fifteen, I began riding at Frank's Chado Farms, I had a junior hunter named Sky High. I still remember that first lesson. As I said, Frank is a man of very few words. Some of the words I recall from that day were "sack of potatoes," "lazy," and "weak." After this encouraging initiation I was invited to come back, and ride the young horses, and to "go to work on my seat."

That was how I was introduced to Frank's training methods for horses and coaching methods for riders twelve years ago. My very first horse show with Frank was equally memorable. I rode one of his horses in a jumper class, and I thought I had done pretty well. Then Frank went in after me and beat me. In fact, for quite a while, I would go in a class and put in a good round, then Frank would go in and beat me. If there is one thing people say about Frank, it is that he is an aggressive rider. I learned to be aggressive from him. After watching him go in the ring after me and beat me so many times, I learned to shave those tenths of a second off my time.

Frank has been an instructor, a parental figure, and an important role model for me. His influence during my formative years as a rider and as a person is immeasurable. Frank has been far more to me than a person to answer my questions. He's been a friend and someone to admire and respect. The way I teach, the way I ride, and the way I approach life reflect his influence.

I found early on that Frank's knowledge is much deeper than anyone else's I've ever come across. It's more than just horse sense. Frank has taught me how to gain the competitive edge on and off horses and he's done so as much by example as by his words. When I'm at a show, he won't say anything about my rounds in five of the six classes I jump. If I have a stop at a jump, he'll say that was fine. If I practically fall off, he'll say that was fine. As long as he knows that I understand the mistakes I made, he won't criticize me. Frank may not say a lot, but, when he does, you know he means it and you know what he suggests needs to be done.

He also taught me to think for myself and he knew when to leave decisions to me. In the final jump-off for the silver and bronze medals in the 1988 Olympics, Frank left the strategic decisions in my hands. I had to decide whether to go slow for a clean round, or to go medium fast, which is what I did. Frank did his job in explaining the technical aspects of the course to me, but the decision to keep kicking, which proved to be the right choice, was left in my hands, knowing Gem and the horse I was jumping against.

Even now, with an Olympics, a World Equestrian Game, and other international experience under my belt, I continue to learn from Frank. He may not be standing at the in-gate of every one of my classes, but I know he watches me ride whenever he can. His opinion is still very important to me.

It has become a sort of ritual for Frank to stand at the in-gate and say two things before I go in: "Just let him go clean," and "If you do what I say, you'll win."

If there is one thing that I've learned about Frank over the years, it is that he is usually right. So read this book carefully and know that even if his methods seem a bit unconventional at times, they really do work. Remember, if you do what he says, you'll win.

Preface

I have spent my entire life working with horses. I have certainly had many thrilling successes, especially during my years riding for the United States Equestrian Team, but I have also had many failures. I hope what I have learned in the process will help other riders to perform better and to keep them from making some of the mistakes I made.

Remember, it is very hard to make a good horse but it is easy to ruin one. My hope is that the suggestions in this book will guide other riders to give their horses their best chance for success. If this is so, then writing it will have been well worth the effort.

Chado Farms   Frank Chapot
August 1992

1

How I learned to win

The early years

*A*t the age of nine, while my classmates in sub-urban Mountainside, New Jersey, were spending their free time playing tennis and baseball, I was busy with my first business venture involving horses. And, while it had noth-ing to do with the show ring, like many other paths I've fol-lowed in my life, it eventually led there.

My entry into the world of horses came with a little Welsh-crossbred pony named Snapper. My father, an amateur horse-man who enjoyed weekend pleasure riding with my mother, Dorothy, bought Snapper and a cart for me at an auction.

I began earning spending money by hitching Snapper to the cart and selling soft drinks near my home on a Union County

Park route that led toward the Watchung Stables, a boarding and lesson establishment. Once there, I watched people school their horses, take lessons, and compete in small shows.

Most of the riding I did in those days was by the seat of my pants. I had some lessons from time to time from local professionals, but I had very little formal training. I picked up most of what I learned by watching other people and through trial and error.

I'm not quite sure where I picked up the aggressive, forward style I ultimately developed. However, I was always competitive, and when I went to the shows at Watchung and saw the other kids riding in jumping classes, I wanted to try competing too. The jumping classes then were not as technical as they are now; by and large, it was twice around the outside with an occasional triple bar in the center of the ring. It's hard to imagine anyone competing successfully at the major shows today without some formal training.

I did very little significant showing until after World War II, when I was about twelve. I became more seriously involved in the sport after my father bought me my first horse, a wonderful gelding we called Chado. Chado was often champion or reserve in the open working hunter division, and he was my equitation mount as well. When I was fourteen, with Chado's able assistance, I won the ASPCA Maclay Finals at the National Horse Show at Madison Square Garden in New York.

At about the time I won the Maclay, I went to a horse show with my father where I was tied for the championship in the working hunter division. The tiebreaker was a hack-off. Although it looked to me like the other rider's horse was running away with its rider, she won the championship. When I said to my father that this seemed unfair, he replied that there is only one division at a horse show where results are objective and not based on someone else's opinion: the jumpers. My father's advice made a lot of sense to me. Thus, with my foundation established in hunters and equitation, I progressed to the jumper ring.

In the 1950s, most of the classes were rub classes, with penalties deducted for a horse touching a rail, even if it didn't fall. In those days, poling—rapping a horses leg's with a bamboo pole—was a common practice to sharpen a horse and teach it not to hit

Frank Chapot, age fourteen, competing in a hunter class on Chado at the Piping Rock Horse Show in Long Island. This duo won many championships in the open working hunter division. (Frank had been wearing a hunt cap in this class, but it had fallen off.) (Photo by Carl Klein Photo)

Winning the ASPCA Maclay finals at the National Horse Show, New York, in 1947, on Chado. (Photo by Carl Klein Photo)

the jumps. However, the horses that were poled frequently tended to stop, and it took a strong, aggressive rider to get them over the jumps in the schooling ring prior to the class. I started getting rides because I managed to get the horses over the schooling jumps without a stop. There was no secret formula to my ability to do it. I was determined to do my best and gave the horses a forward, aggressive ride.

In those early years, one of the best horses I rode was Royal

Knight, a Thoroughbred by Bonne Nuit owned by the late Norman Coates of Far Hills, New Jersey. You needed a very careful horse for those rub classes, and the Bonne Nuit horses seemed to have a terrific dislike of hitting the jumps, which made them very special. (I eventually used the Bonne Nuit lineage as the foundation of my breeding program.)

On this horse and others, I got quite a bit of mileage in the jumper ring. I continued to show jumpers while I attended the Wharton School at the University of Pennsylvania in Philadelphia, and after my graduation, when I enlisted in the Air Force.

As I developed as a jumper rider, I was lucky enough to learn from Bill Steinkraus, who had a reputation as a successful rider of many champions at the national level before he joined the United States Equestrian Team in 1951. His observations on my technique helped me improve; I also benefited from watching how he rode and what he did to win.

Having been fairly successful in the jumper ring up to this point, I decided to try out for the 1956 Olympic show-jumping team. When I applied to the Air Force for permission they transferred me from Lackland Air Force Base in San Antonio, Texas, to Tryon, North Carolina for the trials. Little did I know that my hardest lessons in learning to win were still ahead of me.

Riding for the Team

In the late 1950s and early 1960s the United States Equestrian Team was very much a closed shop because of the differences in competing in the United States and internationally. It was like going from playing baseball in the minor leagues to playing in the majors. Team riders participated in a rigorous training program to prepare for international competition. Once you got the international mileage, it was hard for someone else to bump you off the team who didn't have that experience. Consequently,

Bert deNemethy, shown here longing a horse over cavalletti. Bert's longing techniques are famous throughout the world.

once you were chosen for the Team, you stayed on for a long time, which is not usually the case anymore. Also, when I tried out, there were not many riders seeking a place on the Team. Now, there is a larger pool of capable riders eager to ride for their country. I didn't expect to be selected, but I got a break when the horse of nationally known rider Charlie Dennehy was injured, and I was selected to replace him.

The horse I rode in the trials and in the Olympics was Belair, a horse I owned that was blind in one eye. Belair's bad eye did not affect his ability to get over the fences. (I've never seen a horse with only one functional eye have a problem jumping. However, with today's emphasis on speed and turning, a horse with impaired vision could be at a disadvantage in a tight turn towards its blind eye.)

That summer, on the way to the Stockholm Olympics, I got

my first taste of international competition. I also met someone who had a profound influence on my riding: Bertalan deNemethy, a Hungarian Cavalry officer who emigrated to the United States after World War II and became our coach and chef d'équipe in 1955. Bert introduced me to dressage and cavalletti work and through the dressage techniques he taught me, I learned to sit more deeply and to create impulsion from behind when it was

Bert deNemethy, the master from whom we have all learned so much.

needed. I also learned to include cavalletti training in my program for schooling jumpers. I was never a stylist, but Bert taught me the fundamentals of good flatwork.

One of our first stops on this international tour was Cologne, Germany, for a friendly international competition. My fellow teammates were Bill Steinkraus, Hugh Wiley, and Warren Wofford. The first time I saw a puissance class was at that German show and, frankly, the size of the jump, 6' 7", awed me. What really impressed me was that after six or seven horses had jumped an obstacle of that size quite easily, the competition was stopped because the riders wanted to save their horses for the upcoming Olympics.

One of the ways I expanded my equestrian knowledge in Europe was by watching the other competitors. Observing other riders is an excellent learning tool. You can see what they're doing that works and what doesn't. Piero and Raimondo d'Inzeo, two brothers on the Italian Team, were influential in developing my technique, as was Hans Günter Winkler, a German rider. Winkler, who rode in an authoritative German style, communicated to his horses every move he wanted them to make, and those horses were so well schooled that they responded immediately to each of his commands. I especially remember watching him ride his famous mare Halla. Now, though, I don't completely agree with Winkler's exacting methods. I think, as the d'Inzeo brothers did, that you should recognize that your equine partner has an eye of its own when jumping and allow a good horse to have some role in the decision-making process.

While I was in Cologne, I rode in a speed class and went clear. I thought I was going quite fast, and expected a good placing. Was I ever wrong! I placed fifteenth. Right then and there my fellow Team members and I realized that we had to figure out what techniques the Europeans were using that made their horses perform so much better than ours. If we didn't, we would continue to be left in the dust.

The answer to our big question was painfully obvious: The horses ridden by the Europeans were better trained and prepared than ours. I remember telling Bill Steinkraus, "If we stay here the rest of our lives we'll never win anything." It was very frustrating. Among the lessons we needed to learn was how to take the shortest route on course and how to shorten and lengthen our horses' strides more smoothly.

I came to Europe not really prepared for the type of competition I faced. The Europeans were able to handle the courses, jump-offs, and speed competitions better than I could because their horses had been trained to be more responsive and their riders had far more international experience. Once the U.S. Team realized what needed to be done to get us on a par with the Europeans, we got to work with Bert, continued our European tour, and picked up quite a bit of international competitive seasoning in the bargain.

Every week, we had to play a new game in a new location. In Germany, we had to jump high and wide over elaborately decorated fences. In Italy, the courses were tricky, with very tough combinations and distances. In England, we had to be extremely careful because the fences came down with a light touch. France was somewhat of a mixture of the other three. It was quite an education.

At this point, I started to analyze what questions the course was asking and how to ride different horses with different problems over these courses. I realized that this was the best way to approach a course.

At the 1956 Olympics in Stockholm, I rode Belair, Steinkraus rode Night Owl, and Wiley rode the Team's Trail Guide. Wofford was the alternate rider. It was evident that our early efforts, our techniques still needed refining. We placed fifth. But as our long, hot summer came to an end, we shook off that dust we had been left in and began to win some of the European classes.

With these hard-learned lessons under my belt and a few

Bill Steinkraus on Fleet Apple displaying his impeccable style. It is hard to find a picture of this great rider (an Olympic individual gold medalist) where he is not in perfect form.

more years of exposure to international competition, I was far better prepared for the 1960 Olympics in Rome. There, I rode Trail Guide. I was joined again by Bill Steinkraus and by George Morris, who was a newcomer to the team. We were pleased to bring the team silver medal back to the United States.

Shortly after returning home from the 1960 Olympics, I became acquainted with the Fenwick family in Maryland, who were involved with steeplechasing. Being a naturally competitive person, I thought this sport would be fun to try. As in show jumping, it helps in steeplechasing to be able to find the shortest route over the course. By saving a little ground here and there, you can sometimes beat a faster horse if its momentum has carried it into a wider turn. I thought my show jumping background would help me here, and it did to some extent.

The point-to-points and hunt meets in which I rode were not held on a conventional racetrack with a rail on each side. Instead, they were—and still are—held in an open field or group of fields with some sort of beacon or flag to mark the turns. Keeping a galloping racehorse in close to one of these beacons and tight around the turn was not as easy as I'd thought, but I did not give up and was lucky enough to win some races. I rode over hurdles and brush, but found it difficult to maintain the low weight required for these races, so I ended up riding mainly over timber. One of the highlights of this phase of my career was winning the Invitational Championship Point-to-Point in Middleburg, Virginia, on a horse named Russ, owned by J.L.B Bentley. I also finished third twice in the Maryland Hunt Cup. I

On Bold Minstrel, Bill Steinkraus jumps the Irish bank at Hickstead (England) in perfect form. Bill, who has never been a fan of the "crest release," shows the classic straight line from the horse's mouth to his elbow. (Photo by Jean Bridel of L'Annee Hippique)

was not as lucky in the Virginia Gold Cup: I started twice and fell twice.

While riding in steeplechases was not one of Bert deNemethy's favorite training methods for a show-jumping rider, I did learn quite a bit. There is always something to be learned from good horsemen, no matter what their discipline. I gained knowledge about care and conditioning, as well as riding. One lesson I still use today is to ride forward to a fence and let the horse's own eye guage the take-off spot. Too many riders are so worried about finding the perfect distance that they disturb their horse's rhythm and concentration. In a race, arguing with the horse in front of a fence can have disastrous results. In the show ring, the minimal result could be a stop or a rail down.

Besides learning more about going forward, I enjoyed my steeplechasing days very much. Competing head-to-head with other jockeys in a race was a very different experience from going in the ring by myself to jump a course. It was exciting and lots of fun. In those days, riders didn't specialize in one phase of equestrian activity as much as they do now. People fox hunted and steeplechased and played a little polo and showed. Now, jumper riders tend to have no other focus. Some people who show jumpers do not even show hunters. It may be better this way, but it was more fun in the earlier days.

I continued to ride for the Team in each Olympic competition through the 1976 games in Montreal. In addition to riding in six Olympics, I represented the Team in ninety-eight Nations Cups, fourty-six of which we won, and in other international classes. My Nations Cup record was cited as the most successful in the *Guinness Book of World Records*. One of the highlights of my competitive career was winning the King George V Gold Cup Trophy riding Mainspring at the Royal International Horse Show in London and accepting the trophy for that victory from Queen Elizabeth II. That same year, I placed third in the World Championships at Hickstead, England.

Frank Chapot receives the King George V Gold Cup Trophy from Queen Elizabeth II at the Royal International Horse Show in London in 1974. (Photo by E.D. Lacey)

They say all good things must come to an end, and in 1976 I decided to give up international competition. I was ready to give the up-and-coming young riders a chance for a place on the Team. I was also ready to focus more attention on my breeding program at home and on other facets of the show-jumping industry, including training, instructing, judging, and course design. To be successful in the show-jumping business, it helps to diversify a bit.

I concluded my Olympic jumping career at the 1976 Montreal Games with a fifth-place individual finish and a fourth-place team finish on Viscount, a talented horse loaned to me by the Raymond Firestone family. My last international class that year was at the Royal Winter Fair in Toronto, where I and my fellow team members placed first in the Nations Cup as we had done, earlier that fall at the Washington International Horse Show and National Horse Show. It was a memorable last season riding for the Team; what I didn't know then was that my affiliation with the Team was far from over.

A new role on the Team

In 1980, Bert deNemethy retired from his role as trainer and chef d'équipe of the Team. I began functioning as chef d'équipe some time afterwards, but my role was a bit different from what Bert's had been. By 1980, because the sport and, therefore, the riders had become so much more sophisticated, there was no longer a demand for a full-time Team trainer. Most Team riders these days have their own trainers or are trainers themselves. I still advise the riders who need it, and, as part of my duties, I plan the Team strategy.

Since 1980, I have served as chef d'équipe through three Olympic Games: at the 1984 games, where the show jumping squad won a team gold, an individual gold, and an individual silver medal; the 1988 games where they took home the team silver medal and an individual silver medal; and at the 1992 games where they won an individual bronze medal. In the 1986 World Championships in Aachen, Germany, I coached the Team to a gold-medal finish. I also have been chef d'équipe in several Nations Cup and World Cup competitions.

It's always special to see those you have coached do well, so it has been very rewarding for me to see the successes won by Greg Best and Gem Twist, a horse I bred and trained. Greg and Gem won the individual silver medal in the 1988 Olympics; they then went on to the 1990 World Championships where Gem

Frank and Mary Chapot at the Dublin Horse Show.
(Photo © Irish Times)

Twist, who is owned by Michael Golden of Chester, New Jersey, was named best horse.

My role as chef d'équipe has been both rewarding and challenging. But while the job is certainly demanding and time-consuming, it still leaves me more time for my other show-jumping interests—including judging, course designing, riding, and training—than I ever had while riding for the Team. I've been fortunate enough to have the opportunity to judge or design courses for some of the major shows in this country, among them the National Horse Show, the Pennsylvania National, Devon, the International Jumping Derby, and the Pan American Games.

I've also been able to devote time to help my wife Mary Mairs Chapot train our daughters Wendy and Laura. Mary and I met when she successfully tried out for the Team in 1961. She was a member of the 1964 Olympic Team in Tokyo on a great mare named Tomboy. In addition, Mary was the first woman to win a gold medal at the Pan American Games when she rode Tomboy to win the team and individual gold in 1963. We married in 1965 and were both members of the 1968 Olympic Team (Mary rode a horse named White Lightning that was bred by her mother). In addition to riding and training, Mary has focused her efforts on coaching Wendy and Laura to become winners in equitation, junior hunters, and junion jumpers—and, in recent years, in amateur-owner and open jumpers. Wendy and Laura have done most of their winning on our homebreds, all of whom are from the Bonne Nuit line, as is Gem Twist.

Meanwhile, I continue to ride, compete, and, most important, to learn. I learn from the horses, from my students, and from the people I see and meet at shows and elsewhere. I believe you never stop learning until you're in the grave, and I hope to be around for many more learning experiences.

2

Choosing a winning horse

Once a rider has decided to focus his or her efforts in the jumper divisions, the next step usually is to find an appropriate horse. When a horse is suited to its job and well matched with its rider, success at the horse shows, while not a given, is a far more likely possibility. There are many ways to select a good horse, many places to look for such a horse, and many considerations to think about before embarking on a search for the horse that will be right for your goals, your level of expertise, and your pocketbook. My approach is not the only one; however, it has worked for me over the years and has resulted in my acquiring some very useful jumpers for myself, my family, and my students.

Locating an appropriate horse can seem overwhelming, especially to an inexperienced buyer. To avoid making a costly and perhaps dangerous mistake, a novice buyer should seek professional help both in looking for a horse and in training it.

A few pointers before you shop

When I am looking at a horse to buy, I take into consideration conformation, temperament, and, of course, ability. A fourth very important consideration is the horse's present level of training and ultimate potential, which need to be measured against the rider's goals and ability. Certainly a horse that I would ride can be less experienced or more difficult than one for a beginning adult-amateur jumper rider.

Before you look at a horse, you need to establish its age, experience, size, level of fitness, and any available past history. Although I generally don't feel that a horse's size is a major factor, it may be if you are bigger or smaller than average. A short, lightweight rider may find it difficult to control a huge warmblood. Conversely, a tall, heavy rider may overburden a small horse.

When shopping for a horse, don't count on being able to fix every problem you see in a prospective purchase. It's very easy to be fooled into thinking, "If I just do this one little thing differently, I know this horse will be better!" Assume that what you see is what you get, and if you can be happy with that, buy the horse! If the horse does get better, which it may, that's a bonus. As a seller, I sometimes encounter self-professed "experts" who believe that under their special training program, my horse will be much better. Selling a horse to this type of buyer is very easy.

Conformation is not everything

When people ask me what type of horse I prefer—the Thoroughbred or the warmblood, a smaller horse or a bigger horse, or a gelding or a mare—I tell them I prefer a horse that doesn't like to hit the jumps. Great jumpers come in all shapes, sizes, and breeds. Ironically, many of them don't measure up to contemporary show-ring standards of perfect conformation. If you look at conformation photographs of some of the great jumpers of the world, you can find quite a bit to criticize. However, the qualities these equine stars have in common are that they are careful, athletic, and have the temperament and scope to adapt to the various challenges of today's courses.

Dr. Daniel Marks, who has served as the United States Equestrian Team veterinarian through many Olympic Games and has seen hundreds of international grand prix jumpers, has some interesting theories about conformation as it relates to ability. His theories are a bit unorthodox; however, I have found them to be sound. This is what he writes.

"While top-class Olympic jumpers are of diverse types, there are some features of conformation that contribute to their extraordinary ability and also pertain to their soundness. The literature on conformation addresses many of these, but also contains oft-repeated dogma that is disputed by observation.

"The neck is usually set on high coming out of the top of the shoulder: however, the 'peacock neck' of the Saddlebred horse is rarely seen.

"The shoulder blade (scapula), which determines the slope of the shoulder, is usually quite upright and long. The sloping shoulder of the 'daisy cutter' (a horse whose feet move close to the ground) may win hunter hacks and races, but is not desirable for a grand prix jumper. The triceps muscle, which bulges above the elbow, is usually well developed in horses with a

Jet Run. *This photograph, taken while Jet Run was recovering from an illness, does not do this wonderful horse esthetic justice, but it does illustrate his upright shoulder blade, which when rotated, allowed him to use his knees perfectly over a fence. Notice that the point of his hip is very high and well forward, with great length to the point of his buttock. Jet had exceptional elasticity in his loin, which enabled outstanding engagement of his hind leg and also caused a little wiggle to his walk. His long Thoroughbred muscles gave him extraordinary scope, which permitted him to just canter to very wide oxers. As Michael Matz's best horse, Jet Run set a standard for ease and consistency. (Photo by Daniel Marks)*

Idle Dice. *Partnered with Rodney Jenkins, Idle Dice won more and stayed sounder than any horse I have known. Short-backed and 17 hands tall, "Ike" could turn better than any horse to win a speed class, outjump all others to win the puissance, and then win the grand prix, and he did this regularly for many years. His prominent withers, depth through the heart, and upright shoulder are characteristic of many exceptional jumpers. (Photo by Daniel Marks)*

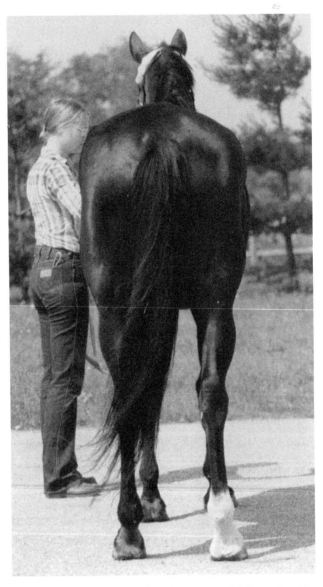

Idle Dice *(hind end). While hip bones this high and wide are not typical of most Thoroughbreds, they are a very desirable feature, and in the case of this Thoroughbred, they gave him great power off the ground. (Photo by Daniel Marks)*

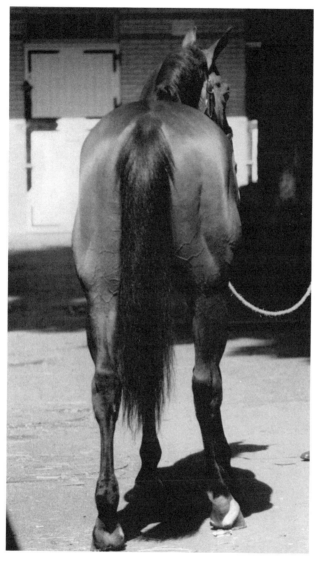

Galoubet (hind end). *This splendid French stallion never had to develop a jumping technique; he had such great power that he merely had to propel his body into the air as high as he wished. This he did with his large and very well-defined biceps femoris muscles, which are visible here, giving width to his stifles. Muscles like this are seen in some of the best warmbloods. (Photo by Daniel Marks)*

Riviera Wonder. *Short-necked, unsound, and with a problem jumping water, Wonder, at his best, was nevertheless the best horse I have ever seen. Deep through the heart, with the longest shoulder blade of any horse I can remember, his front end fairly slammed off the ground, his short back led to incredible agility for a big horse, and his high buttock and obvious jumping bump lent him easy scope. Also he could really buck. This 17-hand son of the great jumping stallion Bonne Nuit combined power, balance, technique, and an aversion to touching fences that was unmatched until Gem Twist, a great-grandson of Bonne Nuit, came along, like a ghost from the past, to remind us of how horses can really jump. (Photo by Daniel Marks)*

San Lucas. *At 17.3 hands, this Thoroughbred was Frank Chapot's mount for jumping really big jumps. They won numerous puissance classes and regularly jumped in the biggest grand prix, Olympic Games, and World Championships for twelve years, and the horse retired sound. Part of this is the result of his inherent soundness and part is due to the graduated system of training and showing that the USET employed under the direction of Bert deNemethy. "Luke" was not an early prodigy, and with his size and length he really needed the dressage and gymnastics that were fundamental to Bert's system. When all this basic schooling came to fruition, the results were truly impressive. He is standing a bit over at the knee, which is a defect only in books, not in real life. (Photo by Daniel Marks)*

Sloopy. *This ungainly Thoroughbred with his upside-down neck, his hocks "in the next county," and a mean streak a mile wide, had prodigious scope. His long croup, noticeable jumping bump, and very high buttocks accounted for this. His long back and loin allowed for extraordinary flexibility in the air. Here we see him recovering from a very serious and debilitating respiratory infection; we knew he was improving when he started to try to bite. Recover he did, and some weeks later gave Neil Shapiro an individual bronze and team silver medals in the Munich Olympics, where he had one of only three clear rounds in the Nations Cup. (Photo by Daniel Marks)*

Touch of Class. *Even with a conspicuous wither she could not make 16.1 hands, but with her elegant face and delicate legs, "Kitty" epitomized the refined Thoroughbred. Many thought her too small, too dainty; they were proved wrong by her two gold medals at the 1984 Olympics—she had only one fence down in that memorable week. In spite of being "light made," she has very well developed hamstring muscles and is long from the point of her hip to the point of her buttock. Her short back assisted her in maintaining the impulsion and balance necessary to negotiate big courses. (Photo by Daniel Marks)*

Gem Twist. *The best jumping horse in the world today—there will be some arguments, but that is my opinion.* *His strong neck coming out of the top of his shoulder, his long upright shoulder blade, his low shoulder joint, his horizontal arm, and his well-developed triceps muscle give him the most explosive front end of any horse I have seen.* *"A bit quick off the ground" was John Whitaker's comment after riding him in the change of riders at the World Championships in Stockholm, where Gem Twist was adjudged the best horse.* *Gem has great depth through his stifles and is also wide through his stifles from behind.* *As an inexperienced horse he and Greg Best won two silver medals at the 1988 Olympics in Seoul.* *Compare this photograph of Gem Twist to that of his cousin, Riviera Wonder.* *(Photo by Daniel Marks)*

Milton. *The all-time money-winning show jumper and a two-time World Cup winner, Milton.* *This halfbred has smashing presence and would be an eyecatcher even without his reputation.* *Beautifully balanced, he can outturn almost any other grand prix horse and can open his gallop to leave out strides.* *His straight hocks would delight a conformation-hunter judge.* *When he was a young horse, his front-end technique left something to be desired, but his hind end was extravagant.* *Ably trained and ridden by John Whitaker, Milton has developed into England's best, possibly best ever.* *(Photo by Daniel Marks)*

Big Ben. *Even Ian Millar looks small on this 17.3-hand giant; but a gentle, lazy giant he is not. Bred in Belgium, Benny's big size, big shoulder, big wither, and high, wide hips combine to give him really colossal ability. But it is one thing to have this ability and another to have the handiness and balance to win grand prix. Big Ben's short back has helped Ian to make him surprisingly adjustable and maneuverable. Such a big horse does not usually excell indoors, but two World Cup wins dispute this. (Photo by Daniel Marks)*

good front end. The arm (humerus) usually tends toward the horizontal.

"All of the best Thoroughbreds have a very prominent wither, but this is not always the case with warmbloods. Occasionally, a horse with a naturally high wither will fall over backwards, causing fractures of the tops of the vertebrae. When these heal, the horse is left with a squashed, flat wither, but it usually has no adverse affect on jumping ability.

"The combination of a prominent wither and a long upright

shoulder blade dictate that the distance from the withers to the girth—the depth through the heart—is great.

"Extremely short-backed jumpers may lack the flexibility to really flip their hind ends, and if they develop back pain, it is usually more debilitating than in longer-backed individuals. Long-backed horses are less handy and harder to keep balanced, but frequently are scopey. However, the modern trend in show jumping favors short backs.

"Although the front legs contribute to the propulsive force of the jump, the principal jumping muscles are the hamstring group, especially the large biceps femoris muscle located behind and above the stifle joint. When viewed from the side, these muscles, when well developed, give depth through the stifle; when seen from behind, they give width through the stifle. These muscles are well developed and bulky in many of the best warmbloods, whereas Thoroughbreds usually have longer, less body-builder-like muscles. There seems to be a relationship between the size of the muscles and the height and width of the hip bones (tuber coxae). Horses with high, wide hip bones do not require great width of muscling through the stifles, but horses with lower hip bones—a more common Thoroughbred conformation—must be wide through the stifles when seen from behind.

"Looking at the top line of the croup, a prominent 'jumping bump' (tuber sacrale) is a frequent feature. This is a noticeable bump on the highest point of the rump (see photographs of Jet Run, Riviera Wonder, Sloopy, and Gem Twist). An extremely sloping croup ('goose rump') is rarely found in the elite today, but, in those few, it is always quite long. In fact, great length from the hip bones to the point of the buttock (tuber ischii) is very desirable. Some of the horses with the most scope have a long, flat croup with a noticeable jumping bump.

"The hip joint, which cannot be seen but must be felt to determine its location, is usually quite high and back in top jumpers, which leads to a long thigh (femur).

"Much has been written about the length of the cannon bones, but observation does not evidence any relationship between this and jumping ability; nor in my experience, does it influence soundness in jumpers.

"Also, the angle of the hock seems unimportant. Some great horses have had very straight hocks, while others have had angulated hocks. Some of the best horses have been base narrow—'cow hocked'—with no adverse effects. The opposite, 'bow legged' hocks, are not seen in this group. This joint is highly stressed by jumping, and horses with weak hocks rarely, if ever, are able to remain sound.

"Pasterns that slope a lot are frequently found in some of the best, and long, upright pasterns are not a significant drawback. Short, upright pasterns, however, usually lead to soundness problems.

"Unlike with racehorses, the conformation of the show jumper's knee (carpus) is of no great import, and jumpers with offset knees or who are 'back at the knee' have been able to jump soundly on legs that would not be able to withstand the strain of racing.

"The feet are vitally important in absorbing the stresses of jumping, and those stellar horses who have poor feet are only able to compete with the care of an exemplary farrier and very good management." *(Extracted from a letter from Dr. Daniel Marks.)*

I don't usually worry about most conformation faults unless I think that the defect in question could pose a soundness problem as the horse progresses in its jumper career. No matter how good a horse is, it is not going to be very useful if it breaks down.

Before you begin to focus on a horse's legs, take a good look at the horse as a whole and try to form a basic impression of how the horse is built. Determine whether its body is in proportion. Is its back short or long? Does the horse stand higher behind than in front? How is its neck attached and does it form a nice picture with the rest of the horse? Although a short back is usually more popular, you may not want to rule out a long back on a horse—there have been many great jumpers with long backs, including Tomboy and Ksar d'Esprit. Do the horse's body parts fit together harmoniously? Does the horse have a good, strong frame? How well the horse is muscled probably should not be a big issue. You may be able to develop muscling, depending on the horse's age and recent training program.

One part of the horse I pay particular attention to is the foot. The jumper goes over many fences in its lifetime, and the feet have to absorb a lot of shock. In addition, horses often have to jump over courses on ground that is hard, stony, deep, or in some way less than ideal. Accordingly, I like a nice, wide, solid foot. However, not many horses have this ideal foot. Although I've certainly lived with horses with shelly hooves, tiny feet, contracted heels, and other foot faults, I'm always happy to see a big, wide foot on a prospect. Years ago, the main source for potential jumpers was the racetrack, and the majority of racehorses had bad feet and light bones. Now, there are many more racetracks where even the slower horses can compete; more drugs are permitted as well. As a result, fewer racehorses reach show trainers than before and, unfortunately, many of these horses are not very useful at all.

For the same reasons you want good feet, good bone is important. A horse with a substantial bone structure will probably withstand the physical stress of jumping better than a horse with a lighter bone structure. However, the jumper candidate need not have a leg as thick as a telephone pole.

Although many professionals want to see a horse with a straight hind leg, I've seen some very good jumpers with the biggest sickle hocks you'd ever want to see. Also, I usually am not too concerned about a horse that is over at the knee. While unacceptable in the conformation-hunter divisions, these horses are often the last to break down. Calf-kneed (back at the knee) horses have the opposite flaw and are not quite as acceptable because they have a greater tendency toward injury. An overly straight pastern angle is also less desirable than a properly angled one. Certainly, a straight leg is preferable to a crooked one, but I had one filly foaled at my farm with a really crooked leg that is now middle-aged and still showing successfully as a jumper.

Many leg problems that would bother others don't bother me. For example, a horse with an old bowed tendon may not be able to return to the stress of racing, but properly rested will probably stand up very well to the strain of show jumping. Capped hocks also should not affect a horse's soundness, nor should windpuffs or old splints. Similarly, an old set curb, while unsightly, usually does not cause many problems.

Visible blemishes and faults can occur in varying degrees and ought to be evaluated by your veterinarian before you turn down a promising horse. Several types of problems, such as ringbone, sidebone, navicular disease, bone spurs, and fractures will show up on X rays. These should be evaluated by a veterinarian familiar with your goals. Depending upon how you are going to use your horse, you may be able to live with some of these problems. However, if you are going to be taking a lot of lessons and showing often, your horse will have to be more durable than one that will be lightly ridden and shown. I'm not a veterinarian and chances are, neither are you, so if you really like a horse that seems to have a few blemishes, get your veterinarian's opinion. Don't lose a good horse without first consulting an expert.

The size of a horse is an issue that's vastly overrated. Nearly everyone wants a big horse, but there are plenty of small horses out there that are wonderful jumpers. The good big horse may be better than the good small one because of strength and a naturally longer stride. However, I never regretted buying Good

Jappeloup, the 15-hand "pony," was big enough to win the Olympic gold medal in Seoul in 1988 with French Team member Pierre Durand in the irons. (Photo copyright © Tish Quirk)

Twist, a stallion decidedly on the small side. Clearly a giant like Big Ben is a superstar, as was San Lucas, but that special big horse is very hard to find. Many are too big for their own good. If a clever little horse has enough scope and a long stride, it can jump with the best of them. Horses like Good Twist, Jappeloup, and Touch of Class have been very special little horses in their own right.

Good Twist and San Lucas are examples of two very talented horses I was lucky enough to ride that were opposites in size. Good Twist, the foundation sire of my breeding program and the winner of many international classes, was only 15.1 hands tall. Many people would have overlooked him because of his size. I was fortunate enough to see him jump in Florida as a three-year-old with Kathy Kusner (who rode for the Team in three Olympic Games). He easily left out a stride in a two-stride combination in a jump-off, convincing me he certainly had the talent to be a special horse.

Frank Chapot riding Good Twist in an international jumping class at the National Horse Show, New York, 1972. Perhaps Frank's best-known mount, Good Twist became the foundation sire for his breeding program. Among the many talented jumpers sired by this 15.1-hand grandson of Bonne Nuit is Gem Twist, silver-medal winner at the 1988 Olympics in Seoul.

Frank Chapot riding San Lucas over the puissance wall at the Royal Winter Fair, Toronto, 1966. (Photo by Budd)

At the other end of the size spectrum, San Lucas, my mount in two Olympic Games, stood well over 17 hands. His one flaw was that he wasn't very fast. He could make turns as tight as any horse, but he was hard to hold together on an open galloping course, which sometimes would result in rails down. However, he was brave enough to jump seven-foot walls in the puissance classes, and he was careful and athletic enough to win the President's Cup indoors at the Washington International Horse Show as well as many other honors.

The well-bred jumper

A few years ago, there were few sources for jumpers in this country other than the racetrack. It seemed then that there was an inexhaustible supply of sound, slow racehorses, and as a result very few North American horsemen thought much about breeding their own jumpers. Also, with the high number of racetrack rejects available, breeding jumpers was not often a profitable venture. Even today, the chances of breeding a super-star are few and far between, and the odds of breeding a whole string of superstars are virtually nil. Europeans, however, have been breeding show jumpers for years and have several estab-lished "families" that have produced numerous wonderful jump-ers. Because they lacked the easy supply of Thoroughbred horses we once had in this country, the Europeans bred their horses from big, heavy driving-horse breeds; these were commonly called "coldblooded" horses. More recently, those horses have been crossed with Thoroughbreds to produce the contemporary warmblood, which, at its best, combines the heart and fire of the Thoroughbred with the strength and steadiness of the so-called coldblood.

As a result, there are now many good bloodlines to consider when looking for a young, unproven, prospect. While not a guarantee of stardom, it is certainly a plus for a young horse if its pedigree includes some names you recognize. Many great jumpers trace their bloodlines back to well-known Thorough-breds such as The Tetrarch, Teddy, Roi Herode, Nasrullah, Man O' War, and Blenheim II, among others. I have had particular success with the Bonne Nuit line and am always interested in looking at relatives of that Thoroughbred, no matter how dis-tant. Well-known bloodlines in Europe include Thoroughbreds and warmbloods: Lucky Boy, Alme, and Furioso, to name only a few.

The right mix

A suitable temperament is of utmost importance in the horse you select; it is also one of the hardest traits to gauge. Bert deNemethy's statement about temperament is all too true: "Difficult to judge at first glance but even more difficult to change, a horse's disposition is an important factor in his suitability as a jumper." I couldn't agree more. By temperament, I don't mean only whether the horse will bite or kick in the stall, but also whether it is going to be willing to jump and try hard, or whether it is a bit sulky. Most important, you need to know whether the horse is tractable enough to adjust to the different questions it will be asked on course.

These days, courses are far more sophisticated than in the past. Course designers don't build just for power and scope anymore; they test the rider's ability to think and control the horse. Accordingly, you need a horse that will shorten and lengthen its stride when necessary and will react appropriately to its rider's aids. A horse that is a bit high-strung is fine for some, but I would stay away from horses that are too difficult to control or lacking in common sense. The days of the crazy, out-of-control open jumper are well in the past.

A hot horse is suitable for riders who like their mounts to have engines of their own and who can ride with a certain amount of finesse. At the other end of the spectrum is the horse with little ambition that is going to need a strong rider to hold it together and create the impulsion it must have to jump big fences. Clearly, somewhere in between is the ideal. You should have in mind the kind of horse that suits you best before you go on your shopping trip.

An ideal horse for someone just starting out in the jumper division is an older horse just past his prime that is still jumping big courses, but might be happier moving down a notch. You have to be in the right place at the right time to fine this type of

A good case for the older horse with a young or inexperienced rider. This photograph shows my daughter, Wendy, on her mother's horse Sharrar, shortly before his retirement. He is already starting a left-hand turn pretty much on his own. Wendy isn't doing anything to hinder the horse, but she's not guiding him much either. In her favor, she is looking where she's going and her balance for landing is excellent. Sharrar certainly knows where he's going. (Taken in a schooling-jumper class at the Lake Placid Horse Show, Lake Placid, New York, in 1984.) (Photo by Pennington Galleries)

horse, and while they are usually not inexpensive, these horses are well worth the price. They know the game and are not apt to make green mistakes. Instead, they have the scope and mileage to cope with the rider's inexperience. They also know all the tricks when going against the clock. With proper care, an older horse can last a long time. A rider can gain invaluable experience from this schoolmaster and have fun in the bargain.

A less-than-ideal combination is a green horse and an inexperienced rider. The old adage that green and green don't make blue clearly makes sense, because both horse and rider are going to make mistakes. If this situation is unavoidable, an inexperienced rider should have professional help in selecting and training a green horse.

Many people are opposed even to considering purchasing a mare. However, Mary and I have had terrific luck with mares. Among the top jumpers Manon, Tomboy, White Lightning, and Anakonda, we have had quite a string of them. Good ones are admittedly hard to find, but if you have one, you have something special. I feel the same way about stallions. If you have a good one, he will give you that little bit extra sometimes that might make the difference between winning and losing. Geldings are usually more docile and easier to handle than either stallions or mares.

Besides finding a horse with a good disposition and common sense, you want to find one that does not like to hit the jumps. That is why I have always liked the Bonne Nuit line. Numerous descendants of Bonne Nuit had just the right mix to be great jumpers. Many of them went on to be Olympic horses, including Miss Budweiser, who won a team bronze medal in the 1952 Olympic Games in Helsinki with Arthur McCashin; Riviera Wonder, the great horse Bill Steinkraus rode in the individual competition in the 1960 Olympics in Rome; Night Owl, Steinkraus's mount at the 1956 Games in Stockholm; Out Late, our reserve horse at the Olympic Games in Mexico in 1968 with

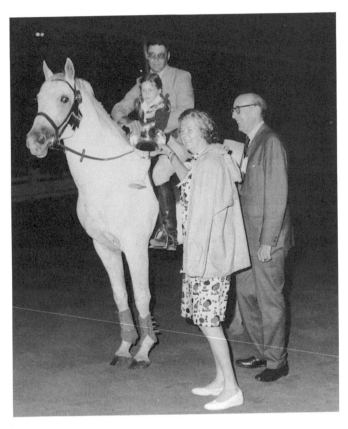

An example of a well-behaved stallion. Good Twist winning the USET Stakes at Devon. The presenters of the trophy are Mr. and Mrs. Whitney Stone; the extra rider is Wendy Chapot.

Carol Thompson; and, of course, Gem Twist, who was ridden by Greg Best to an individual and team silver medal at the Olympic Games in Seoul in 1988. This is a pretty impressive list for one bloodline.

Finding the right mix of temperament is essential. What I've learned over the years is that a good jumper is what I call a mixture of bravery and chicken. The horse must be brave enough to jump and chicken enough to want to avoid hitting the jump.

If you put too much bravery in the mixture, the horse won't care about hitting the jump. Or, if you put too much chicken in the mixture, the horse will stop. The key is to find the right combination, and enhance it.

Temperament is one of the most difficult traits to assess when looking at a prospect, particularly since you often don't know what kind of preparation the horse has had prior to your arrival. You should notice if the horse is excitable or spooky, especially if it is on its home ground. Decide whether you can deal with the horse as it is that day. Never be so sure of yourself that you think you can change what you see in front of you. I do not like to see a horse that pins its ears back and sulks at the rider's leg. That sort of behavior can only cause problems in the future. Keep in mind your level of riding; if you are very experienced, you can manage a horse with a more difficult temperament than if you are just beginning to ride jumpers.

Trying the horse

While conformation is important as it relates to a horse's soundness and performance potential, and temperament is important as it relates to the horse's ability to learn and respond to the rider's aids, a horse's natural enthusiasm for jumping and athletic ability over a fence are the most important factors to consider when selecting a jumper.

When the seller brings his or her horse out under tack for you to see, pay attention to the type of equipment the horse is wearing. If you buy the horse, you may want to use the same selection. Does the horse wear boots because it hits its ankles or merely for protection? Is the horse wearing a martingale and, if so, how tight is it? What kind of bit is being used? Are there any extra pads under the saddle? Is the rider wearing spurs? If the horse is wearing something out of the ordinary, do not be afraid to ask questions, and don't be afraid to ask for a different bit if you are uncomfortable with the one the horse has on once you are riding it. You might as well find out right away that the horse does not like your favorite bit, rather than when you get the horse home. However, do not subject the horse (and the seller) to a drawn-out lesson on your training methods. That is not really fair, especially if you do not buy the horse.

When watching a horse go on the flat, you want to see a horse with straight gaits, a long-enough stride to cover the ground well, and a springy step. I usually find that if the horse has a spring to its gait, it has a spring to its jump. You want to see a light, free mover, but not necessarily a "daisy cutter" that could go out and win an under-saddle class. The brilliant movers on the flat, while beautiful to watch, don't always pull up their knees very well over the fences. Although I'm never one to say that a jumper has to pull its knees to its chin, it has to be somewhat athletic with its legs. The spectacular mover that can also snap its knees way up over the fences is worth a fortune in the hunter ring.

Years ago, when the courses were very simple and vertical, some Standardbreds made good jumpers. We even used large Hackneys with a lot of knee action. They made great jumpers because they pulled their knees out of the way so well. Today, however, they would not have the scope to handle the spreads and long distances.

When looking at a prospective jumper, notice its training on the flat. Does the horse know its flying changes, and can it do them in both directions? Can it lengthen and shorten its strides on the flat? Also, watch the horse on a circle. Is it willing to bend, or is it belligerent and stiff? Can it hold its lead and balance at the canter on a small circle?

Naturally, the bottom line is how the horse jumps. If you have

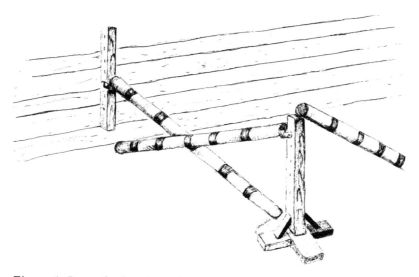

Figure 1. Jump for longing. (*Drawing by Jackie Promaulayko*)

a young, green horse that hasn't jumped much, try to free school or longe it. Put a rail alongside a low standard so the longe line slides over it (see figure 1) and set up a low jump no more than 1-$^1/_2$ to 2 feet to start with, working up to maybe 3 feet if the horse has jumped a little before. Don't ruin someone's nice unbroken young horse by jumping it too high the first time it has ever seen a fence. Also, do not be fooled by watching a horse jump loose. Don't think you are getting a world-beater if the horse jumps like a gazelle without a rider. The graceful gazelle you see as a light two-year-old may become a moose when it matures to full size and has a rider on its back. The European dealers sell a lot of horses this way, but I have some qualms from a buyer's viewpoint.

When looking at a young, green horse, I don't mind if it is cautious or suspicious about new jumps and stops every now and then. I also do not mind if it isn't perfect with its knees over the low jumps. In fact, the horse that's pretty with its knees over

Here is a young horse with great ability, not impressed with the low jump he is being asked to negotiate. This fence is no challenge, so he does not fold his legs well.

The same horse, over a bigger, more challenging jump. Notice where his legs are when asked a more difficult question. (Photos by Mary Chapot)

little fences may be close to the limit of its ability, while the horse that doesn't bother to tuck its legs over a crossrail may be the "scopiest" thing you ever sat on, once it starts jumping obstacles of a more challenging size. If a horse refuses a jump, try to assess whether it stopped because it was put into an impossible situation or if it has a stopping habit. If possible, move one of the jumps in the ring or change the face of one, and see if the horse is brave enough to jump. Watch the horse's ears. I worry about a horse that stops at a fence with its ears pinned and a sour expression.

When you start to jump the horse you are trying, the seller will probably show you what the horse does best. Again, don't worry if the horse is not using its knees well over the low fences. However, the prospect should fold its legs evenly and not hang one leg down. You want to see the horse take off lightly and jump the smaller jumps without a big effort.

Don't be put off if a horse knocks down a rail. If that happens, pay attention to what the horse does the next time over the fence. Does it just hit it again from carelessness? Does the horse twist and squirm and seem afraid? Or does it jump in wonderful form and much higher over the fence? It's not hard to figure out which scenario you should like the best.

After I've seen a horse jump, I like to vary what the seller is showing me by moving the fences to shorten long distances or lengthen short ones, if I have not been shown both. Then I set a correct distance to a fence I can build up. Again, I evaluate the horse's temperament as it jumps. Does the horse get excited, does it hurry, or does it really need to be kicked along and clucked at to get down the line? If the seller does not have a specific plan and just tells me to go ahead and try the horse any way I want, I often work with an in-and-out. Depending on the horse's training level, I may start with a crossrail to a small vertical (soon to become an oxer), that can be trotted comfortably. I try to start with distances that are easy for the horse, so I can watch its form and ease of motion; I try not to trap it. I like to work with a combination of a vertical and an oxer, one stride apart, jumping it both ways and changing the inside distance to test the horse's scope as well as its ability to shorten and lengthen its stride. By doing a figure eight over the "out" of the in-and-out (see diagram and detailed explanation of this exercise in Chapter 3) you can test the horse's ability over single fences, as well as its willingness to turn and its general "ridability." You seldom have a whole grand prix field on which to try a horse, and this little exercise has worked well for me. This drill also works well if you are trying a horse at a show, where space usually is limited to the schooling area.

If you are looking at a prospect at a show, watch the horse every time it goes and, above all, be sure to watch it in the schooling area before it goes in the ring. Note the warm-up immediately before the horse goes in the ring and, if you can, see whether it is ridden or longed earlier in the day. If you like what you see in the ring, you may want to follow the same procedure if you buy the horse. Again, don't be fooled into thinking that you will be able to make major improvements, you may, but don't count on it.

The final step in shopping for the right horse is to have it examined by a qualified equine veterinarian. The days of a veterinarian "passing" or "failing" a horse outright are waning. Now, the veterinarian is more likely to tell you what he or she finds, such as navicular changes or an old fracture, and then advise you as to whether you can live with those problems, depending on how you're going to use the horse.

With all this advice, finding the right horse is not an exact science. I also think a little bit of luck is involved here, but careful and deliberate shopping can increase the odds of finding the horse that suits you and your goals.

3

Doing your homework

Getting started—a brief overview

*W*hen you've chosen and brought home the horse you hope will forge a winning partnership with you, the next step is to establish a solid working foundation. Whether you bought an older, experienced horse or a younger, green prospect, you need a good program specifically tailored to your horse. Developing an appropriate work plan and slowly and carefully preparing yourself and your horse will ultimately pay off at the horse shows. As in any field or discipline, those who do their homework conscientiously are more likely to go to the top of the class.

Naturally, the program you set up should be based on the requirements of your horse and your goals. You need to consider the horse's temperament, level of fitness, and training. (A horse with a nervous temperament will require a different program than the quiet or sluggish animal.) Generally, I have found that the warmblood must be quite fit, especially at the grand prix level, while the Thoroughbred can do with a little less conditioning. Set up your program with a goal in mind, whether it is preparing for an upcoming horse show, accomplishing a certain schooling exercise, or getting around a particular course smoothly. Doing so will make your riding more satisfying and more entertaining. Remember, however, that a horse is a live animal. If things don't go as you expected, don't be too rigid in following your plan. Instead, try changing what you've been doing for a while, but be sure to remain flexible to meet your horse's needs.

A training program for a jumper should include plenty of flatwork. You want to teach your horse all the skills it will need to negotiate a course of jumps, keeping in mind that it's the ability to adjust between the jumps that produces the most successful rounds. Just as the flatwork you do depends on what your horse needs, your jumping program should also be tailored to the horse's requirements. An experienced horse does not usually need much jumping at home, except before a show. A green horse, on the other hand, needs to learn to use itself over the jumps and almost always benefits from a program that includes cavalletti, gymnastics, and courses—usually over jumps set at about 3 feet.

For a change of pace, try doing some flatwork outside the ring. One of the best exercises for improving a horse's balance and getting it fit is trotting up hills. If you live in an area with hilly terrain, take advantage of that resource. Trail riding offers most horses a pleasant diversion and can be a great help in relaxing the hot horse. This type of horse can also benefit from long, relaxed walks and plenty of time off, preferably turned out in a field or paddock. When weather conditions permit, I've found that it's often helpful to turn the tense horse out at night, too.

Like most workers, horses benefit from time off the job. Horses should have at least one day a week without work and should spend as much time as possible turned out. Most horses benefit from living as close to their natural state as they can, so I prefer to keep horses outdoors as much of the day as is feasible. Before the winter circuits became such an important part of the horse show world, my horses would have their shoes pulled in December and spend the winter months outdoors in paddocks with run-in sheds. In those days, the horses would come back refreshed and ready to work after their long winter break.

Saddles, bits, and other equipment

When it comes to bits and bitting, less is usually better. However, a 90-lb girl riding a 17-hand horse probably would need more bit than I would on the same horse. As a horseman, I like to use as little bit as possible, but I'm not against using the more severe bits for control, when necessary. A rider on an underbitted horse cannot ride effectively. The horse pulls and the rider pulls back and the result is unpleasant. The rider winds up using strength instead of technique. As anyone who has tried pitting his or her strength against the strength of a horse knows, it's a losing battle.

When figuring out what bit to use, start by trying your horse in a plain snaffle. If you feel you need to switch to a stronger bit, first determine how severe a problem you have. Is the horse a little strong, or is it actually running away with you? A twisted snaffle may be the answer for the horse that is a little strong, while the serious puller may require a twisted wire snaffle. A dropped noseband or figure eight noseband can be useful for the horse that pulls and opens its mouth as well. It is amazing what a difference closing such a horse's mouth rather firmly with a noseband can do to help with control.

There are literally dozens of bits in the tack shops to try, from copper mouthpieces for the dry-mouthed horse, to roller bits for the ones that play with their tongues, to rubber bits for sensitive mouths, and so on. There is also a wide variety of pelhams from which to choose. A straight-bar pelham works on the bars of the horse's mouth and is often ideal for a horse that likes to stick its nose out too far. Others just will not tolerate this bit at all.

It's easy to amass a whole trunkful of bits, hoping to solve all your training problems with a new bit. Sooner or later, though, you may have to go back to basic riding techniques and spend some time teaching the horse to respond to your commands. A solid training foundation goes a lot further than most bits and other "quick fix" devices.

Some riders find the gag a useful bit for horses they can't otherwise hold. Although the gag is popular in Europe, especially among the French riders, I prefer not to use it. The gag sits high in the horse's mouth and functions as a pulley, increasing the strength of the hand. This bit tends to raise a horse's head, and I can think of very few circumstances when I would want a bit to have that effect. Like any severe bit, the gag also tends to lose its effectiveness if used too often. Therefore, if you must use one in the show ring, try not to use it for everyday flatwork and schooling over fences. I'm often surprised to see people riding with a gag and draw reins at the same time. It makes me wonder what they are trying to do, since draw reins are usually used to lower a horse's head while a gag bit raises it.

An elevator bit and the currently popular three-ring bit work in a similar manner to a gag. One of the drawbacks to a gag is that the pulley is often sluggish, which results in a late response to the rider's hand. The elevator and three-ring seem to function more smoothly, but they are still not on my list of favorites.

I've seen the hackamore, which works by exerting pressure on the nose or jaw, used with great success. The most notable examples I can think of were two highly successful European horse and rider combinations. One was German rider Paul Schockemöhle and his famous horse Deister, who were European champions three consecutive times. The other was Irish rider Eddie Macken and Boomerang, who still hold a record with four consecutive wins in the British Jumping Derby. The hackamore, which comes in different types, is a useful device for horses that are so sensitive that even a light feel of their mouths with a normal bit causes them to fuss with their heads. I'm not at all opposed to the use of the hackamore for the horse that won't accept a bit.

Part of becoming a horseman is figuring out what works best for you and the horses you're riding. If someone uses a bit I personally wouldn't choose, but is successful, I certainly would be the last to criticize.

A novice rider with uneducated hands should use a less severe bit and a light rein contact. I don't like to see a rider approach a jump with loose reins, but I prefer that to seeing the rider unwittingly pull on the horse's mouth. If in doubt, you should let go.

Draw reins, which help position the horse's head and influence balance, should be used by very experienced riders only and should not be used all the time by anyone. When I was training with Bert deNemethy, he compared the use of draw reins by a novice rider to a knife in a monkey's hand. I have to agree. In addition to their potential danger, draw reins used too often can become a crutch the rider leans on to solve problems. Ironically, the draw reins can also become a crutch for the horse. The horse that once leaned on your hands may very well find a new place to lean; right on those draw reins. When using draw reins, I do not like to have them so tight and rigid that the horse

Here is a rider using draw reins incorrectly. They are too tight and allow no freedom for the horse's head and neck. (Photo by Jackie Promaulayko)

never gets any reward for putting its head where I want it. One of the advantages of draw reins is that they can be adjusted to suit the situation. The horse should only come into contact with the draw reins when it gets its nose too high or too far out. When jumping with draw reins, you need almost double the release over a fence than you would otherwise.

A standing martingale can be effective in correcting a head-carriage problem. For an inexperienced rider trying to lower his or her horse's head, this piece of equipment is a far better choice than draw reins. The martingale should be adjusted so that the horse only feels it when the horse puts its head or nose in an unacceptable position. I do not like to see a martingale so tight that the horse is not allowed any freedom at all. While I do admit there are some horses that need this restraint, they are thankfully few and far between.

Standing martingales are not allowed in the FEI (Fédération Equestre Internationale) disciplines, so I don't use them on my horses that compete at those upper levels. However, I regularly use standing martingales as the need arises on horses competing in classes not governed by the FEI and would not mind using them on upper-level horses if the rules were changed. I certainly would support such a rule change. A standing martingale is less abusive than other equipment riders tend to substitute for it.

This is how draw reins should look on a horse when used correctly. Notice the slack in the rein, giving the horse freedom if its head is in the proper place. The draw reins only come into play if the horse raises its head. (Photo by Jackie Promaulayko)

A running martingale works off the reins and, consequently, the horse's mouth, somewhat like draw reins. Like draw reins, a running martingale shouldn't be adjusted so it is always in effect. Instead, this piece of equipment should be set so it only comes into play when the horse puts his head in an unsatisfactory position.

The type of saddle I prefer offers as close a contact as possible with the horse. I strongly dislike heavy padding for this reason, but for a horse with a sensitive back, a big, fleecy, protective pad is a necessity. I don't like a saddle with a high cantle because it makes me feel like I'm on a carousel.

For the horse's legs, I prefer boots with an open front so the horse can feel the jump if it hits it. I don't use bandages to protect a horse's legs because of the chance they could come loose and cause an accident. I've seen too many horses go around a course while one bandage is slowly unwrapping and getting tangled in the other legs. Also, a bandage put on unevenly or too tightly can cause major injury to the very leg it is there to shield. For protection of a horse's coronary bands, I often use bell boots, especially when competing on grass on a horse wearing studs on its shoes. I have had only one horse that would not tolerate the bell boots flopping around on her feet. Most horses do not mind them. If a horse hits its hind ankles, some sort of ankle boot is a must. Otherwise, I would not use anything on the hind legs.

In most cases, a rider should carry a whip and wear spurs on a regular basis. If you are not used to carrying a whip, it will feel awkward at first, but you will get used to it. If your horse is afraid of a whip, be careful and don't wave it around. Your horse will get used to the whip, too. If you wear spurs regularly, you will soon learn the difference between correct and incorrect use from the way your horse behaves. The spur should come into play only when necessary. If you let your toe point out too much, you are going to stick the spur accidentally into the horse at the wrong time. Instead, ride with your foot parallel to the horse's side. If you find yourself gripping with your calves, and ultimately the spurs for security, get someone to help you, and spend some time on the longe line riding without stirrups until you relax your legs and find your balance in a more natural position. Ideally, the rider should put on spurs and carry a whip as naturally and as comfortably as he or she puts on socks in the morning.

Flatwork

Good basics on the flat are an essential ingredient in the making of a jumper. Today's sophisticated courses require a strong foundation of dressage-related flatwork. When I think of dressage for jumpers, I'm not thinking of the difficult movements required of a grand prix dressage horse. However, the basic principles of dressage, which call for the harmonious development of the horse and rider and include the goals of balance, calmness, and flexibility, certainly apply to the training of all horses.

Working properly on the flat teaches the horse to carry the rider's weight and enables the horse to be supple, to turn well, and to adjust its stride between the fences. Ultimately, as I learned while competing in Europe, the horse that is adjustable and can turn efficiently will almost always beat the horse that can't.

I prefer to do concentrated flatwork with my horses for a short time each day. For the average horse, twenty minutes a day of concentrated work at the trot and canter is enough. If you have a horse that's a slow learner or a horse with a difficult temperament that needs more time under saddle, it is much better to work the horse twenty minutes twice a day than forty minutes once a day. Because very few horses can tolerate the physical and mental stress of forty minutes of strenuous flatwork at the trot and canter, the extra time is at best not effective and at worst, can result in injuries that would only set back your program.

Working with a former racehorse may require a different approach, at least initially, because of the way these horses have been ridden. If you are working with a horse from the racetrack, remember that its back muscles are not used to carrying the full weight of a rider for very long. On the contrary, the racehorse is used to carrying a rider who probably spent much of the time standing in the stirrups with his weight off his mount's back. It is likely that the horse has balanced itself on its forehand, leaning on the rider's hands. You need to spend some time doing slow, easy work while the horse finds its natural balance and its back muscles gradually get stronger. Occasionally, you will find a horse that is so naturally well balanced that it does not get on its forehand at all. If that describes your situation, be happy, because you can then skip the extensive flatwork most former racehorses need to learn how to balance themselves. Your prospective jumper needs to learn to use its hind end, because this is the source of a good jumper's balance and strength. This process should be done very slowly and carefully so you do not put too much stress on those undeveloped muscles. If you rush, you will do more harm than good.

When you first come out of the barn with your horse, give it a chance to loosen up before doing any concentrated work. A horse's muscles need to be warmed up before a workout, just as with an athlete. Some horses need more time to warm up than others. A stiff, older horse may, for example, require a longer loosening-up period than a younger one. When you start, let the horse relax and walk for a while. At the trot, don't ask for much collection, and don't sit down and ask the horse to accept your weight until its back muscles have loosened and the horse goes forward in a relaxed manner. At this point, the horse is ready to begin serious flatwork at the trot and canter.

While working at the trot and canter, include some transitions in each direction. These transitions improve the horse's adjustability and balance. Go from a working trot to a strong trot and back to the working trot; then go from the trot to the canter and back again. From a halt, go to a working trot or canter and back to a smooth halt. Use both a sitting trot and a posting trot and make your transitions on a circle as well as on a straight line. You should also make backing an element of your flatwork program.

An efficient working canter can make all the difference in the world since the canter is the jumper's working gait. If you want your horse to be a jumper, don't canter it around in a dull, listless manner, as you would in a bridle-path hack class. That type of canter is fine only for a pleasure class. For a jumper, you need to practice an active canter. When you're cantering, ask yourself, "How high can I jump from this canter?" If the answer is, "I have enough horse underneath me to jump 5 feet," then you're practicing a useful canter.

Jumpers can benefit from doing lateral work. The shoulder-in, the haunches-in, the two-track, and leg yielding are very good exercises to teach your horse flexibility and obedience. These exercises teach the horse to move away from the rider's leg, which is a necessity on course, especially in a jump-off. However, do not force your horse to do any of these movements too long. At best, the horse will be bored. At worst, it will become angry and resentful. If the horse does not perform a lateral movement exactly right, do something different and then come back to the lateral exercise with a fresh perspective. Sometimes, you have to settle for an inch of progress instead of the mile you had wanted. When starting to teach your horse lateral movements, begin them at the walk and then progress to the trot and perhaps to the canter (if your horse gets really good at them).

Your horse should be able to do a turn on the forehand and a turn on the haunches. I frequently use the turn on the haunches during routine flatwork because it gets the horse's balance on its hind end and is the first step toward a rollback turn at the canter.

I like to use several exercises to teach a horse to turn. One I call "concentric circles," in which I canter the horse on a large circle, gradually spiraling inward until I am almost doing a pirouette. This maneuver requires a strong leg since the horse will slow down a lot as the circle gets smaller. Then, I increase the circumference of the circle until I am cantering on a large circle again.

Another exercise I use is the rollback. I start this exercise by cantering the horse down the straight side of the ring. Then, at a predetermined place, I ask for a half-pirouette back to the other direction, canter a few more strides, do a flying change, and then do the same thing in the other direction. Start practicing this exercise at the walk, then at the trot, then at the canter, and finally at the gallop. When you can execute this maneuver successfully on the flat, add a rail on the ground before your turn and another after, and make the rollback between the two rails. Ultimately, you can make the rails into small jumps.

Doing rollbacks is not an exercise for a green three-year-old, but most well-schooled horses seem to enjoy it. While many horses start out a little sloppy, they usually catch on fairly quickly and can soon perform rollbacks out in a field without a rail as a guide.

Turning correctly is crucial for the jumper. With placings decided by mere fractions of a second, your turns can make the difference between a high placing and none at all. Think of pushing your horse around the turns with your hands and outside leg, rather than pulling it around. Your inside hand gives direction while your outside hand keeps the horse's out-side shoulder from going in the opposite direction from the turn, which will make your turn better and quicker. Bert deNemethy used to tell me to think of the reins as sticks in my hands and to move them together in the direction of the turn. Direct the front end but don't pull or you will lose your forward momentum.

Jumpers need to know how to make flying changes in order to remain balanced when switching direction. Most horses learn to do them pretty naturally as they go around a course. Others have to be taught. Ultimately, most jumpers do them automati-cally. They know that they will be making a right turn after a jump when there is a wall on the left and no place to make a left turn. At that point they will automatically change to the right lead. It is a form of resistance when you are cantering down the center of the ring and want to go left but the horse will not change its lead.

There are many ways to teach a horse flying changes. Many jumper riders like to teach this maneuver over a very low jump or rail on the ground. Approach the rail or obstacle on an angle, and just as you get there, change the direction of your horse's head with your inside hand and the bend of the horse's body with your outside leg. That is the signal for the horse to change its lead. Another way to teach the flying change is by cantering on the counter lead. When you get to a turn, you have the horse hold its counter lead, which makes balancing difficult. Then you ask for the flying change. Most horses are happy to comply since it is easier to balance when on the correct lead, especially on a turn.

Once your horse learns the flying change and can do them in both directions cleanly and without becoming disunited, I wouldn't practice it very much. Asking a horse for too many flying changes can make it tense. In the final analysis, you want your horse to be thinking about the jumps on course, not the flying changes on the approach. After all, your horse will not be judged on its changes in the jumper division as it would in the hunter division.

The counter-canter, or canter on the off lead, is a good tool to improve obedience and balance. I sometimes think of it as an extension of leg yielding because in both exercises the horse must move away from the rider's leg. It is not natural for a horse to canter in a circle to the left on its right lead. To do this, the horse has to bring its hind end underneath itself or lose its balance and fall. When doing the counter-canter, be careful not to use so much hand that you give the horse a place to lean. The horse should remain balanced on a light contact.

Vary your routine on the flat to keep it interesting for you and your horse. Change direction often and perform each movement you do in both directions. Many horses are more comfortable going in one direction or the other. Some horses will resent feeling or obeying the rider's leg on one side more than the other, or will be stiff and heavy on one side. Learn to recognize this, and deal with it by using some of the previously mentioned suppling exercises.

I'm often asked where the horse's head should be positioned (see photos). When working on the flat, I like to see the head fairly close to the vertical with some flexion at the poll. I take into consideration the horse's natural conformation, and try not to ask a horse for a head position that is totally unnatural for it. This would be uncomfortable for the animal and nearly impossible to maintain while jumping. I also consider age and experience when thinking about head carriage. I do not ask a young, green horse for as much flexion as I might a more mature horse. When working with a horse, don't get so focused on what the head is doing that you forget the overall balance, especially the hind end. After all, head position is only part of the whole training picture.

Horse overbent; too much collection.

Horse not collected at all. Its head is too high.

Horse's head in the correct position.

Cavalletti and gymnastics

Cavalletti or rails on the ground can be used as a tool to improve balance. They also can be used to develop muscle, teach lead changes, and improve adjustability without the stress of jumping. A small minority of horses never learn to relax over cavalletti but the vast majority do.

I like to start with two cavalletti since the horse will be more likely to jump a single rail on the ground rather than to trot over it. I place the cavalletti about 4 feet to 4-1/2 feet apart, adjusting the distance so it's comfortable for the horse's stride at a working trot. Start by walking the horse over the cavalletti so it will relax and then move up to the trot. Work up to four rails on the ground or try the grid I designed (see figure 2 and the photographs) to allow for a variety of options with the rails in a compact area.

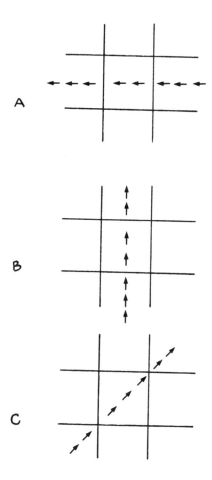

Figure 2. Cavalletti grid design. The cavalletti are placed about 4 to 4½ feet apart, depending on the length of the horse's stride.

When you are using the grid, notch the rails so they won't roll when the horse goes through. (This is especially important when using the upper pair of rails.) Start by riding your horse over the rails resting on the ground. When the horse trots over these in a relaxed and forward manner, in both directions, try going over the rails resting on the bottom rails. This line of rails makes the horse work a bit more because it has to raise its legs higher.

Cavalletti grid that can be used in several different ways (see figure 1).

Close-up showing notches in rails.

Another close-up showing notches.

(Photos by Jackie Promaulayko)

The easiest way to trot the cavalletti, because the rails are on the ground and, therefore, very low.

The second hardest way to trot the cavalletti, because the rails are about 6 inches off the ground, making the horse exert more effort when stepping over the cavalletti. This is an example of a horse reaching into the cavalletti, instead of adding an extra step. (Photos by Jackie Promaulayko)

The hardest way to trot the cavalletti, because the horse must be exact; it can't wander. (Photo by Jackie Promaulayko)

Again, I would go in both directions until the horse trots through nicely. When the horse is going through this line straight and smoothly, you can try the third track over the grid, which is at an acute angle. On this track, the horse must be in front of your seat—going forward willingly in a straight line without excessive use of your leg—and listening to your aids so it's not drifting right or left. To do this line correctly your horse should take only one step in the center of the grid and then step out. Change directions each time you go through, using a figure eight pattern. If you can manage this difficult cavalletti exercise, I would say you have mastered your cavalletti skills quite well.

You can use rails on the ground in a variety of patterns to teach your horse different skills without jumping every day. For example, you can canter over a single rail in a figure-eight pattern to work on turning skills and flying changes. Two rails can be set at angles to each other (see figure 3) and ridden in a figure-eight pattern or straight across to sharpen a rider's eye and turning skills and to improve the horse's adjustability. Rails set in a line as an in and out can be rolled closer together to practice a "tight" distance and further apart to practice a long one. I make relatively narrow cavalletti from old broken rails. They do not take up much room in a small ring, and it can be a challenge to get a spooky young horse over them.

The natural progression from cavalletti is to small jumps and then small jumps in gymnastic combinations. You can accom-

Figure 3. Two rails set at angles to each other can be ridden in a figure-eight pattern or straight across.

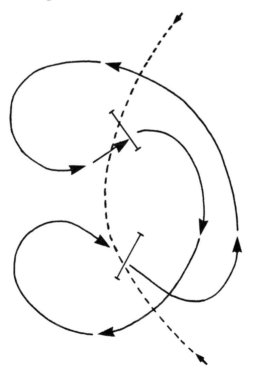

plish most of your needs in schooling the jumper without raising the jumps much higher than 3 feet on a regular basis. Start by making the distances very pleasant and normal. As the horse progresses, make the distances more challenging. Gradually shorten some distances to teach the horse to shorten its stride. Make others long, so the horse learns to lengthen its stride.

The correct way to measure distances between fences is from inside standard to inside standard. For example, if you are measuring the distance between two oxers, measure from the back standards of the first oxer to the front standards of the second oxer. The average horse's canter stride is twelve feet long. When setting your gymnastics, remember that a number of outside factors can affect the length of your horse's stride. The slope of the ground makes a big difference. You will find distances riding much tighter going downhill than uphill. Also, a small ring or a tight turn preceding a line of fences will make a distance seem longer. Deep or slippery footing will make a horse's stride seem shorter.

Not all horses have the same length of stride. Some have a natural eleven-foot stride, while others easily cover thirteen feet. Your job is to assess your horse's stride and if it is longer or shorter than average, to try to teach the horse to adjust to a more normal length with the help of gymnastics. For a prospective jumper, it is much better to be in the position of having to shorten the horse's natural stride rather than lengthen it. The horse with the naturally short stride may lack the scope to jump the bigger fences.

If you have access to a sand ring or a ring with footing that shows hoofprints clearly, you can learn a lot about your horse's stride. Start by raking the sand ring so the surface is smooth. Measure the jumping distances on the basis of a twelve-foot stride but include some combinations with long distances and some with short distances. Make some of these jumps verticals and others spreads. Then ride your horse over the fences and

look at the hoofprints in the sand to see where the horse takes off
and where it lands. You may be surprised to find that your
horse lands closer or further away from the jumps than you'd
expected. When you are at a show, knowledge of where your
horse takes off and lands will help you walk the course and plan
your ride more accurately.

As your horse progresses, you should analyze and try to
correct any problems it may have. For the horse that doesn't pull
its knees up or use its shoulders well, a bounce or no-stride
combination is a very good tool. The bounce is a gymnastic
combination in which the horse jumps in over a jump and jumps
out over another jump without taking a stride in between. I like
to start horses over this type of gymnastic with the fences set
low. A crossrail to a low vertical is a good beginning point. I
usually set the distance at 12-1/2 feet, but I tailor it to the stride of
the horse I'm riding. Ride to a bounce with a little pace. Don't
pull the horse up coming to it. Go forward.

Horses normally learn to jump through bounces very quickly.
Once your horse gets comfortable jumping the bounce with a
crossrail to a vertical, change the bounce to two verticals. When
your horse is confident jumping this, add a third bounce jump,
which should be a small oxer. The oxer can be either the first,
second, or third element of your bounce combination, or all
three for that matter. When using an oxer, you may have to
reduce the distance within the bounce by about six inches because the center of the horse's jumping arc will be over the
center of the oxer. The horse will land closer to the back rail of
the oxer, so he will need less room to jump out. An oxer is an
important element to use in a bounce gymnastic because it makes
the horse use its shoulders.

When setting a distance through a bounce gymnastic, don't
make it so tight that the horse doesn't have room to pull its legs
out of the way. The horse learns very quickly going through a
bounce to use its legs. If the horse jumps too high going into the

bounce, it will penalize itself by hitting the second fence. Once a horse realizes that it will be penalized for jumping high, it will make a smaller jumping effort but pull its legs up more tightly. If the horse does not catch on and keeps jumping in big and hitting the second fence, you'll need to adjust the distances or you'll take the heart out of him (that's why you need to tailor the distances to your horse). Chapter 5 includes a diagram of four progressively difficult bounce grids to try as your training progresses.

A basic setup for your ring

You don't need a grand prix course in your backyard to teach your horse the fundamentals of jumping. In fact, with only six jumping standards, you can teach your horse many lessons in preparation for the jumper ring. Figure 4 shows two very basic setups that can be used for some fundamental exercises to practice shortening and lengthening your horse's stride. Set up the fences as a vertical and an oxer to be jumped from either direction. You can set either a one-stride or a two-stride combination. You can make a small course out of this exercise by jumping the second fence in this combination as a single fence in a figure eight pattern and then going straight through the combination. Practice jumping from the vertical to the oxer and from the oxer to the vertical. For the one-stride combination, set the distance somewhere between 23 and 26 feet, depending on the size of the jumps. If you're starting with your jumps very low, start with a 23-foot distance between the fences. For a two-stride combination, set the distance somewhere between 34 and 37 feet, depending on whether you're practicing a tight or long distance and whether your jumps are large or small. When the jumps are very low and the distance is tight, you can either trot in the first fence and canter out over the second or canter both fences. Don't

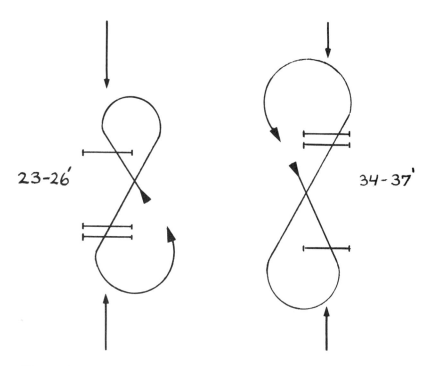

23-26'   34-37'

Figure 4. Two examples of the basic setup with six standards. Distances for a one-stride in-and-out can be anywhere from 23 to 26 feet. Distances for a two-stride combination can be anywhere from 34 to 37 feet, depending on whether you want the distance tight or long, and on the size of the jumps.

just jump the fences straight across the middle. Practice jumping on an angle as well. This is actually an easier way to find a comfortable take-off spot. If you're getting too close, you can open the angle. If your distance is too big, you can close the angle.

If you have just two more standards you can add a third jump to this exercise. Place it at an angle to your combination (see figure 5) so that you can ride it as a broken line. If you have the space, set it at a distance from four to six strides away from the in-and-out. Depending on your track from the combination to the single fence, practice adding or leaving out a stride. When you want to leave out a stride, take the short track from the inside corner of each jump. When you want to add a stride, follow a longer track from the outside corner of the fence. Straightening out the broken line as you stay to the inside makes it easier to leave out a stride, while adding a bend to the line toward the outside gives you more room to add a stride. If you can add yet one more pair of standards, this third jump can become an oxer. Do this exercise in both directions.

Figure 5. Two separate exercises using an in-and-out to a single fence. The distance possibilities are unlimited, depending on your purpose. On the left side you have a vertical-oxer-vertical exercise, and on the right, an oxer-vertical-oxer exercise. Each exercise may be jumped in either direction.

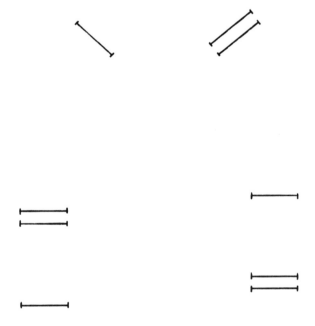

With these exercises, you will be teaching your horse and getting some practice yourself in solving the problems you might encounter in the jumper ring. Some of the options you can try here can be quite difficult. For example, it is very hard to go from a tight combination to a single fence and leave out a stride. It is even more difficult to do the opposite: leave out a stride from a single jump to a tight in-and-out. In practice, I prefer leaving out the stride to a single fence, rather than to a combination, especially for a novice horse or rider. It gets the rider and horse in less trouble.

When you acquire more standards and rails, you can graduate to the next exercise (see figure 6). Here, you have a lot of standards and are putting more lines in the center of your ring.

Figure 6. A further expansion of the previous exercise, which may be jumped in innumerable ways.

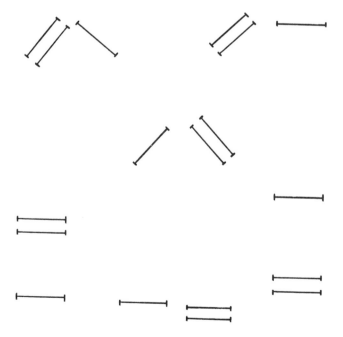

4

Going to
a horse show

Extending your training program at a show

Once you and your horse are working comfortably at home and are making some progress in your training program, it is probably time to go to a horse show, even if not to compete. I like to take my young or newly acquired horses to horse shows early on to give them a chance to take in the hectic and exciting atmosphere. Although your horse may not be ready to show, riding the horse around the grounds and allowing it to become acquainted with a new environment will allow you to concentrate on other problems when the two of you are actually ready to go in a class.

Don't be discouraged if your horse walks off the truck and seems to forget everything it has learned at home. Many horses become excited just by hearing the announcer speak, while others act as if it were part of their daily lives. Although some horses adapt right away, the majority will find the wealth of other horses and high level of activity, among the various other distractions, a big change from home. While ex-racehorses in particular may have a problem with the commotion, the announcer, the crowds, and the general noise level of a horse show can also be very disconcerting to a horse used to quiet surroundings. Try to let your horse see as many parts of the horse show as possible, including the judge's stand, the schooling and show rings, the stabling areas, and the spectator tents. When deciding how much to do with your young horse at a show, use common sense and assess how the horse reacts to the surroundings. If it copes well, you might try a low-level class or two. Otherwise spend the day simply sitting on your horse and letting it see the sights.

Know your limits. If you run into a problem that is beyond your ability to solve, you may need to get help from a professional or a more experienced trainer or rider. You don't want to allow your horse to get away with too much misbehavior—it will only create problems for you in the future. If your horse continually finds it can get the upper hand, it may take advantage of your weaknesses and develop bad habits that will be hard to break. If you are having trouble with your horse it is important to know when to quit doing what you have been doing and get help; continuing to harass your horse sometimes only compounds the problem.

I try to avoid riding a very green horse in schooling sessions held in show rings as these sessions typically consist of a crowd of horses being ridden in every direction and configuration imaginable. This may be too overwhelming for an inexperienced youngster and can do more harm than good if the horse gets kicked or frightened.

Showing a green horse

Once your horse has become fairly comfortable away from home, you may want to start showing it. Even if your horse is going to be a jumper, you might want to start in some hunter classes where you can give the horse some mileage over some low and more straightforward courses. A few years ago, when pre-preliminary and schooling jumper divisions were rare, all my young horses started in the hunter ring. Now, with a wide range of low jumper divisions available, many horses can start right off in the jumper ring. These classes provide an opportunity for your horse to experience a variety of colorful jumps and learn how to turn without being overfaced. If you make it to the jump-off, I recommend not to go too fast. Rather than racing around over low jumps and possibly driving your horse crazy, ride the course at your usual pace, using the jump-off as an opportunity to teach the horse to turn and jump on angles.

You don't need a grand prix course to teach your horse the basics of jumping. Your horse can learn to jump many of the elements of a grand prix course on a much smaller scale. A green mistake over a smaller jump is much easier to rectify than a green mistake when your horse is overfaced. In fact, smaller courses are the best places for horses to learn about different types of obstacles and get used to the different ways jumps are built.

Going to a variety of shows may also give you a chance to compete in an indoor ring. This is especially important if you do not have one at home. Some horses are very uncomfortable indoors if they are not used to it. At large horse shows, stabling overnight provides a new experience for a horse who has never been away from home. It takes a while for many horses to adapt to living in strange surroundings. Simply the fact that the lights are left on all night is a change for most horses.

Two young horses getting some mileage in the hunter ring before going on to the jumpers. Ivorson, a gray, is shown here at Devon, Pennsylvania, in the amateur-owner hunters in 1991 with Laura Chapot. (Photo by Pennington Galleries)

Shindi, a brown, shown here at the Lake Placid Horse Show in 1981 in pre-green hunters with Frank. Both these horses are currently showing in the jumper division. (Photo of Shindi by Reflections of Killington, Gary Coe)

Just as I like young horses to start out showing over low fences, riders should do the same. Here you see my daughter Wendy starting out in the children's jumper division on her pony, Just Sallie, at the Coppergate Horse Show in Basking Ridge, New Jersey, in 1983.

Beginning classes and strategies

Many years ago there were only three open jumper classes in a horse show. As there were no grand prix, the biggest honor was to win the championship. Thus, even though the classes were often diverse (e.g., a rub class, a speed class, and a puissance), the competitors would try to win every class. With the advent of grand prix and speed divisions, people nowadays pick a few classes to enter rather than competing in the entire open-jumper division. While few horses used to specialize in a certain type of class, many horses today compete only in those in which they perform best: some horses may compete mostly in open speed classes; others may be saved just for the grand prix. A horse such as Gem Twist frequently will show only in one or two classes during an entire show. Over the years the focus of show jumping has changed. Now an open-jumper championship is seldom even pinned. Rather, the grand prix is the highlight of the horse show. Therefore, it is important to plan your training sessions and horse-show schedule so that your horse peaks at the right moment.

When planning a show program try to keep your goals realistic and concentrate on the classes that mean the most to you. As with your training program, you will want to keep your horse's level and ability in mind. If you have set a particular goal, plan your training in a way that gets your horse to the competition sharp and ready to win.

A horse show is not usually the time to try something new, whether it is a piece of equipment or a different technique. I learned that lesson the hard way when I bought a pair of breeches before I left for Europe in 1956. The first time I put them on was for the Olympic Games. Before I had finished warming up I had no circulation left in my legs. Bring to the horse show the equipment you know works for you.

When warming up your horse, consider what it needs to get ready to compete. While loosening the horse up on the flat, make sure it is listening to your aids. If your horse tends to get stronger or more excited as you jump more, the less you do the better off you will be. If your horse is spooky you may want to bring a cooler, a coat, or a tarp to hang on the schooling jump. Then if the horse stops outside, you will have a chance to punish it before going in the ring. Many people bring strips of blue canvas to set up as a fake liverpool. These can be helpful to practice over if this type of obstacle is on the course. If your horse is experienced and knows its job, it should not require very much jumping prior to a class. Some of the horses I train, including Gem Twist, jump as few as three jumps before going in the ring.

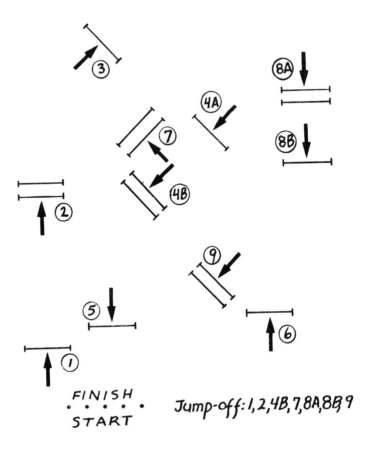

Figure 7. *A simple schooling jumper or low jumper course.*

A typical schooling jumper course

Whether you are starting a green horse or getting started yourself in the jumper division, you will probably encounter courses
with some similarity to the one illustrated here (see figure 7).
While walking the course you will want to keep in mind your
horse's traits. The tendency to jump to one side or to bulge, the
horse's length of stride, and the horse's ability to turn will all

affect how you ride the course. Take a look at the footing and the slope of the ring. While a line may walk in a normal distance, deep footing or an upward slope may make it ride long, and hard footing or a downward slope may make the distance seem short. Frequently you will find inconsistent footing at a show. Being aware of the deep or hard patches will help you determine how to ride the jumps in that area.

When walking a line keep in mind that a horse takes off and lands closer to an oxer than to a vertical. Over an oxer the peak of a horse's jumping arc is in the middle of the jump, whereas over a vertical it is over the rail. Thus, a vertical-to-oxer line, such as 1 to 2 on this course, may ride longer than expected. Look for areas that might be particularly troublesome for your horse. If the horse drifts left or right when it jumps or tends to bulge on bending lines, the lines may not ride exactly as you have walked them. In addition, a more aggressive ride may be needed for a particularly spooky jump. Notice what is outside the ring. Tents, judge's stands, and spectator bleachers set close to the ring may cause your horse to shy away from the rail, making a distance such as that between 1 and 2 longer. Try to keep your horse from being distracted by activities outside the ring, especially around a long turn like that between fences 5 and 6. A line going away from the in-gate may ride differently from a line coming towards home. Because many horses hang back going away from the in-gate, a line such as 1 to 2 to 3 on this course may ride longer than a line in the opposite direction.

Before the signal to begin sounds, try to give your horse as much of a tour of the ring as possible. If there is a particularly spooky jump on the course you should try to ride by it (but don't stop and show your horse the fence as that is cause for elimination). While touring the ring, be careful not to ride through the start markers in the direction of the first fence, even if the whistle hasn't blown. You never know when the judge will give the signal to start. It could be just as you are about to pass through the markers. After the whistle has blown you can only cross the start once or you will be assessed three faults for crossing your path. If the start line crosses the width of the ring (as it does on this course) and you want to get to the other end, enter the ring as soon as the horse before you has jumped the last jump. By crossing the line right away you will minimize the chance the judge will be ready to blow the whistle before you get to the far end.

Note where the finish markers are. While it may seem natural to turn immediately after the last fence and pull up in the center of the ring, don't turn until you have passed through the timers. A finish line a long way from the last jump also provides you with a final opportunity to make up time.

On this course the line from the first to second jump is a normal four strides. As long as you have enough pace to the first fence and your horse does not hang back going away from the in-gate, or spook at one of the obstacles, these fences should not pose a major problem. Fence 3 is set on a bent line to the right. While a rider with a good eye can often judge when to turn as he or she is going to a fence, a less confident rider can find the best path to take on a bent line by walking out different routes. Although the course designer may not have measured this distance, you should plan how many strides you are going to take there. On this course, taking the most obvious slightly bending line from 2 to 3 may get you to fence 3 too tight in five strides. Depending on your horse's length of stride and his tendency to jump to the right or left you might ride directly to 3 in four strides, or bow out the bending line more in five strides. After fence 3 you must roll back to a normal two-stride in-and-out (36 feet). If this course is set in a small ring this turn will become very sharp and you will have to be sure you don't slow down too much around it. If the time allowed is tight, this would be a place to make up some time. In a big ring especially, you don't need to go all the way out to the rail as long as you get straight to 4A and 4B. Because 4A is a vertical and the distance inside the in-and-out is not particularly long, you should not be worried if you don't find a perfect distance to 4A.

Fence 5 is again set on a broken line. Develop your plan for riding this jump as you did for fence 3, considering your horse's stride and tendencies to jump to one side, and how the line walks taking different routes. The turn between 5 and 6 provides another opportunity to make up some time. Fence 6 to fence 7 is another bending line. However, this time these jumps are so far apart (possibly eight or more strides) that I would ride fence 7 off my eye. Fence 8A is probably the most difficult fence on the course. It is an oxer into an in-and-out set quite close to the turn. Here I would go fairly deep into the turn to get straight to the combination. While you want to build up enough impulsion to get over the oxer, you must be careful not to override it and chance knocking down the front rail of the oxer, the out of the in-and-out, or both. Fence 9 is set on a bending line and, as with fences 3 and 5, should be ridden in the way that best suits your horse.

The first two fences in the jump-off are the same as the first two fences in the first round. As you will have more pace in the jump-off, most horses shouldn't have any problem making this distance. In fact, many will find that it will end up tight. Use your experience from the first round to help you decide how to ride this line in the jump off. If the distance was already tight for you, expect it to get even tighter when you are going fast. Although the way the diagram is drawn it does not look possible to cut inside fence 7 to get to 4B, the course designer may have set the jumps in the ring so as to make this option possible. Even if there is room, this will still be a difficult choice. If you select that route, don't let the turn slow you down so much that you can't get over the oxer. Keep up your impulsion and try to ride the turn as smoothly as possible. If you have to zig and zag and slow down a lot just trying to get to the jump, you will lose so much time that you probably would have been faster running around fence 7. To cut inside, your horse must be prepared to turn and jump and should be good at jumping on an angle. You will want to jump this fence at a slight right-to-left angle. However, if the jump is at all wide, you will not be able to angle it as much as if it were a vertical. The more acute the angle on which you try to jump the fence, the wider your horse will have to jump and the greater your chance of having a back rail down. You should practice turns like this at home so you will be able to do them in the show ring. If your horse is inexperienced or you are just in the ring for a school, I would advise going around fence 7. You probably won't win the class, but you will take less of a chance of making a mistake and scaring your horse.

You almost surely will want to turn left to get to fence 7. If this jump were set fairly far back you might be able to make a right turn, but if you jump 4B on an angle to the left, it will probably be faster for you to keep turning left. From the diagram it looks as if you can easily go inside fence 3 to get to 8A and 8B. This is a good opportunity for a very inexperienced horse to try an easier turn. Remember though, that with any horse you must be careful not to start turning before you have left the ground, because your horse, anticipating the turn, may stop. You may have to go a little wide to 8A. If you ride to this jump on a sharp angle, making a tight turn, you will save time, but you will also take a chance of having a rail down and not getting out of the in-and-out in one stride. By the same token, however, you have to take a chance if you want to win.

Depending on your horse's length of stride, you may be able to leave out a stride to the last jump. Again, use your experience from the first round to help select which option to take. If you decide to leave out the stride, you will want to jump the right side of 8B and make the line to 9 as direct as possible. Be definite in your decision. If you are going to leave out the stride, start moving up as soon as you land over 8B. It is much easier to shorten your horse's step, if you see you are getting to 9 too tight, than it is to try to lengthen it at the last minute and ask your horse to leave long.

Many people relax after the last jump, forgetting that on many courses (including this one) the finish is a long way away. Make sure you keep galloping all the way through the markers. To cross the line as close to the last jump as possible you will have to turn slightly left.

This is a nice jump-off for a schooling or childrens/adult class as the riders cannot win solely by speed. The course slows you down by continually making you turn. I feel a course that asks a rider to both run a little and turn a little is the safest kind for this level.

There is no one correct way to ride this course. A variety of strides can be taken on many of the lines, and there are a number of ways to approach the jump off. You should develop a plan for riding this course that takes advantage of your horse's strong points and minimizes its weaknesses.

If you have sufficient equipment, a versatile course similar to this one is nice to set up at home. Not only can it be jumped a number of ways simply by changing the direction of a few lines or by starting with a different fence, but it can also be made much harder or easier by changing the distances or moving the jumps just a little bit.

Don't be discouraged at this stage if everything does not go exactly as planned. An unexpected spook or stop, a missed distance, or some other unintended event may require you to change your plan part way through the course. What is important is to recognize when things are going wrong and be able to adjust your strategy and solve your problems without getting rattled. Don't expect every round to be as smooth as a winning hunter trip. It may take a lot of practice before you and your horse are in synch.

Moving up

There is no fixed schedule indicating when a horse should be competing at a particular level. Horses progress at different rates. While some horses catch on very quickly, others may need more time just to mature enough to handle the questions you ask. A horse's physical and mental age, as well as its ability, play an important role in determining how fast it can advance. Very young horses tend to have a short attention span, making it difficult for them to concentrate for long periods of time. Younger horses also are apt to be rattled more when they make a mistake. Older horses, even if inexperienced, usually are able to absorb lessons more quickly. Nevertheless, if a horse is nine, but still acts like a three-year-old, you probably will have to spend a lot of time with it before it will be ready to graduate to another level. One horse may be mentally ready to advance, but not physically grown up enough to balance itself well, while another may have all the physical components, but not be mentally old enough to move up. Just hitting a rail flusters some horses, while others can knock down three or four rails without being fazed. Horses that are very careful often lose confidence when they make a mistake. These horses in particular should be brought along slowly. They need time in the low divisions to learn how to deal with making mistakes and, as strange as it may sound, to learn to hit a jump without getting totally rattled. We moved Gem Twist up very slowly because we wanted a confident horse in the higher divisions. He tended to overjump so much we didn't want to scare him if he made a mistake.

Some horses constantly are surprised on finding a jump after turning back in a jump-off. These horses are likely to make mistakes until they learn to turn and look for a jump. It also takes some horses a while to get used to jumping an entire course, especially if you usually jump only lines at home.

In general, smaller horses are able to move up more quickly than big horses without getting hurt, because bigger horses tend to take longer to grow into their frames and to learn to carry the weight of a rider and balance themselves. When I first saw Good Twist he was winning classes as a three-year-old, but San Lucas didn't come into his own until he was seven. This is not to say that I would condone the practice of showing a three-year-old, especially over today's courses.

Before you begin to compete over higher jumps you should be able to handle the show courses you are currently jumping comfortably and confidently. Many good horses have lost heart by being pushed too quickly early in their careers. Even a horse

This is a picture of Gem Twist getting some mileage in the hunter division as a three-year-old at the Coppergate Horse Show in Basking Ridge, New Jersey. Later he learned to pull his knees tighter over bigger fences, but you can see even in this picture the buoyant style he exhibits today, overjumping this tiny fence by a wide margin. He is ridden here by Linda Murat, who did much of the early work with him.

with all the talent in the world needs to learn to turn and to adjust its stride over low, even if unchallenging, fences. Teaching the horse these basic skills becomes more difficult as the jumps get bigger. Because there is less room for error, over bigger fences a mistake is more likely to scare your horse than one over jumps that are easy for it.

Give your horse a chance to absorb what you have taught it. Having one successful show in the preliminary division does not mean you are ready to advance to the intermediate. However, if show after show your horse easily handles the task at hand and demonstrates the potential to jump higher and wider fences, then you might try showing in some higher-level classes. On the other hand, you may not have to change divisions to jump more challenging courses; the difficulty of a division's courses varies between course designers, shows, and regions. If you plan to stay in your local area, you may need to move up a division to jump higher jumps, whereas if you will be going to some bigger shows you may be able to stay in the same division. Keep in mind that because of the restrictions placed on entering some divisions, once you show in a higher-level division, you may not be eligible to move back down. If you are competing in the preliminary or intermediate divisions, where winning too much money makes you ineligible, you should plan your show schedule carefully. If you are currently showing over relatively low preliminary or intermediate courses and want to go to shows later in the year where the fences in these divisions will be higher, you may not want to win out of your division too early.

In determining when your horse is ready to move up, you must use some judgment and, most importantly, take your time. No one ever made a mistake by going too slowly. You should never feel pressured. In fact, if you are happy and enjoying yourself at your current level, there is no reason to move up at all. Higher-level divisions tend to be more expensive, especially if you do not win often. Nowadays the lower-level divisions offer a variety of options for riders of all degrees of seriousness and means. These classes enable people who cannot afford an "A" circuit hunter or superstar jumper to show and have fun. If you are only a weekend rider and don't always find the distances to all the jumps, you won't be penalized much in these divisions. While regional high-score awards and classics are available for those who are very competitive and want to show every week, low jumper divisions provide an inexpensive opportunity to compete for those who only want to show from time to time.

5

Solving common problems

*B*y spending sufficient time on the basics and making progress in a slow and careful manner, you will
launch your horse on its jumper career with a strong foundation.
As you advance, drawing on this foundation is the best way to
keep riding problems to a minimum. Yet, even the best horses in
the world have their idiosyncrasies. These quirks need to be
identified, understood, and resolved if you want to form a successful horse-and-rider partnership. Knowing your difficulties
as a rider is equally as important as understanding your horse's
quirks. Here, again, the basics of good riding are the corner-
stones to becoming an advanced rider. For some riders, input
from a ground person from time to time is enough. Others

benefit from taking lessons on a regular basis with a qualified professional.

In this chapter, I will outline some common horse and rider problems and talk about how I solve them. The successful rider has to be an independent thinker because there is so much information that needs to be processed when negotiating a course of jumps. I often suggest to my students that they think of a course as a test of their riding proficiency and of their horse's skill level. A course examines how well you can think, how well you can ride, and how well you have trained your horse. Therefore, to be successful, you need to have a thorough understanding of how your horse behaves on a course. Many people have trainers to help them learn. If you have trouble correcting your horse's weaknesses or your own, you may want to get professional help. I've included at the end of this chapter a discussion of how to find a trainer.

Rider problems

One of the most pressing concerns of jumper riders is seeing a distance to a fence. By distance, I mean a suitable takeoff spot in front of an obstacle. Many riders worry, sometimes too much, about shortening or lengthening their horse's stride to get to that perfect takeoff point. This is a particular concern among riders graduating to a more challenging division who need to be very accurate about riding to higher jumps and more difficult lines. While trying to get to that ideal distance, some of these riders shorten the horse's stride and try to slow the horse coming out of a turn. This practice can have disastrous results, especially if the rider decreases or breaks the horse's stride in the process.

Like their riders, most horses can use their eye to measure a distance. Some horses are better at measuring distances than others, just as some riders are more adept at this skill. When a rider disrupts the rhythm of the canter coming out of a turn, the horse can't use its eye to find the right distance, especially if the rider has broken the horse's stride by nipping with the reins in his or her quest for that perfect distance. On the other hand, if the rider does not interfere with the horse, it can use its eye. At the very high levels of competition, the horse's eye and the rider's eye are in perfect synchronization. That is when every-thing works very well.

The best way to get to that ideal situation is to ride forward out of a turn toward a jump. I do not mean that a rider should gallop wildly out of a turn; instead, he or she should quietly ask the horse to go forward. If you go forward to the jumps, you will see the distances earlier, sometimes four, five, or six strides out. When that happens, you have plenty of time to make any ad-justments several strides away from the fence. For example, if you see a very long distance to the jump, you can encourage your mount to lengthen its stride three or four strides before the obstacle. The same idea holds for seeing a tight distance. If you see a steady distance, you can take your horse back and shorten its stride gradually. When you get to the last stride before the jump, there is nothing, or very little, you have to do. Everything has already been done. The greatest benefit of this approach is that you get to a good distance without upsetting the horse. You won't have to give it a big kick or a jab in the mouth. Ultimately, this style of riding will make your horse quieter and more re-laxed about jumping and improve your chances for success.

Some of the worst riders in the world ride their best when going against the clock: they become more concerned with being fast than with getting a perfect distance, so they tend to leave their horse's mouths alone. Instead of standing in their stirrups, as bad riders often do in the first round, they usually sit in the saddle and push the horse forward during a jump-off as they are supposed to. When a rider is standing in the stirrups, perched on top of the horse, it is hard for him or her to feel the horse's rhythm and see a distance. These same riders are usually at their worst when they are trying to be very accurate.

The question of distance is most important when riding to the first fence of a line. After you have found the takeoff spot for that first jump, distance is no longer as important an issue for the jumps that follow. You will know from having walked the course that it is four or five strides to the next obstacle and three to the next fence and so on. You will also have figured out whether the distance will be long or short for your horse, especially if you followed my recommendation in Chapter 3 and measured your horse's stride. After that important first jump in a line, your eye doesn't have to be terribly accurate to make the necessary adjustments.

Many riders lack a true understanding of the meaning and use of impulsion. These riders do not know how to create impulsion nor how to use it. Failing to create enough impulsion can cause jumping faults such as refusals and knockdowns. I liken this problem to trying to drive a sports car up a steep hill in fourth gear. The tachometer is low, the speedometer is low, and the engine stalls. To correct that problem in a car, you shift down until the tachometer is up near the red line and the speedometer is down, and you get up the hill with ease. In a sense, the horse has an engine, too. If you do not have the horse's engine revved high enough, it makes it difficult for the horse to jump high or wide. To create impulsion, you push the horse forward with your seat and legs, while holding him together with your hands. The seat and the leg create the impulsion, or energy, and the hand controls it by containing it or letting it out. This is a very simple explanation, but impulsion is not as simple to achieve. Finding the correct balance between the legs, seat, and hands is difficult. For each horse, the balance is different. Some horses have more natural ability and require less rider-created impulsion than others. Some Thoroughbreds step out of their stalls with enough natural impulsion to jump a grand prix course. I find that these types of horses, especially if they have decent minds, are easier to ride than many warmbloods because they do not require as strong a rider. Warmbloods, on the other hand, usually need the rider to create the impulsion for them.

A common problem, particularly among less-experienced riders and riders moving up a division, is anxiety. If I am coaching someone who is especially nervous, I try to tell them the show is not that big a deal. After all, if it's not fun, why do it? At the ingate, I might try for a laugh. I always tell Greg Best before he goes in the ring, "Just let him go clean." I have told some students to go in the ring and ride the course as Steinkraus would. That usually gets a giggle.

One phenomenon I happily see very little of these days is the sloppy rider with elbows akimbo and legs flapping, "cowboying" the horse to the jumps. Naturally, there is no penalty in the jumper ring for riding in this manner, but, ultimately, sloppy riding takes its toll. Many young American riders start competing in the jumper division after coming up through the junior equitation and hunter ranks. There, good riding habits are re-

Leslie Burr Lenehan on Jane Clark's Charisma showing the good form she learned as a junior competitor in hunter and equitation classes. She won the World Cup Final and a team gold medal in the 1984 Los Angeles Olympics. (Photo © James Leslie Parker)

Most of the pictures in this book show different riders in a more or less classical jumping position. This photoghaph and the one opposite illustrate other styles that I find perfectly acceptable under the circumstances. The first one shows White Lightning jumping a huge oxer over water in Aachen, Germany (probably in 1972). She is making a big effort, and I am doing all I can to help her make the spread without disturbing her balance. Not a beautiful picture, but effective when the horse needs some help.

warded because they are closely linked to how the competitors are judged. In Europe, where there are few equitation classes, you see more unstylish riding. However, the smooth, quiet European riders are usually the ones who make it to the top. Many years ago, the scenario was quite different. Then, open jumper riders were the buffoons of the horse-show world because of the untidy, casual way they rode. These riders were successful because the courses were far simpler than they are now.

Competing in hunt seat equitation classes provides an excel-

This photograph is an example of what I call a "safety seat." This horse is not going to make it over the back rail of this oxer. I have not interfered with her mouth, nor am I sitting on her back. I am trying to give the horse a chance to jump the fence, but if she crashes, I am in a good position not to get hurt. (Photo by J.J. Walsh)

lent foundation for riding in the jumper division. In fact, I agree with George Morris that these equitation classes could be described as jumper-seat equitation. If you look at upper-level equitation courses, they resemble jumper courses far more than hunter courses (in fact, these equitation classes are often held in the jumper ring). In these classes, the types of jumps used and the distance and riding problems posed, are all similar to jumper courses. The most significant differences between riding the two classes are the added elements of speed and fence height in the jumper class. That is why I think the transition from equitation classes to jumper classes should be smooth and fairly easy.

Reward and punishment—
managing horse problems

Part of the training process is knowing when to punish and when to reward your horse. If your horse stops in front of a fence, it does no good to pat it on the neck. You must let the horse know, in no uncertain terms, that stopping at a jump is unacceptable behavior. On the other hand, if you are training a green horse to jump over water and it finally does what you want, pat the youngster and let it know it did something right.

Stopping does not bother me when a horse is young and/or green and balks at an obstacle it has never seen. You have to determine the reason a horse runs out from a fence or refuses. If the reason is lack of experience, the horse needs more exposure to jumping different kinds of obstacles, or perhaps needs to jump lower obstacles. Many horses stop if they are overfaced or frightened. If your horse is not ready to jump at a higher level, the best solution is to take your time. It takes some horses longer than others to gain confidence over fences. Actually, I would worry about a young horse that was so bold that it would just go down and jump anything without a peek or a run-out from time to time. If a youngster did not stop at an unusual-looking fence occasionally, I would be concerned about how careful this very brave horse would be after it has some mileage and has seen all the different types of jumps used in competition.

When you ride in a major competition, you have to ride your mount as though it is the best horse in the world. You cannot be thinking it is going to stop, anticipating a refusal. If you ride defensively—overriding, keeping too tight a hold of the horse's mouth, or doing anything else to keep the horse from putting on the brakes—you are going to interfere with the horse's performance. You have to believe in the horse and ride it with complete confidence in its ability to jump the fences.

In the days when I was riding competitively on the international level, it was important for me to spend some time away from the horses I rode at home. At home, I would ride all the young, green, and difficult horses. Then, when I rode a horse I was preparing for international competition, I would find myself anticipating the same greenness or behavior problems I was encountering at home. Instead of giving this horse the confident ride it deserved, I would sometimes ride such a horse expecting it to stop, fall, or make a mistake. When I used to leave home on the European tours, it sometimes took me a show or two to get cracking and forget about all the inexperienced and difficult horses I was riding on the other side of the Atlantic.

This was more of a problem with horses I didn't know. I could not help but be confident on some of the great horses I knew well. On Good Twist, for example, I never worried. He was a competitive individual. When he went into the ring, he became a different horse. He puffed himself up and was ready to give the course everything he had.

Pilot error can sometimes cause a refusal, especially if the horse is green. If you feel your riding confused the horse, you can give it the benefit of the doubt. In particular, very careful horses often have a tendency to stop more than less wary animals. However, I would still punish a green horse or a horse I knew was sensitive and conscientious for a refusal. Stopping is simply not acceptable behavior.

Once the horse does stop, you cannot be a nice guy about it. I would never advocate punishing the horse excessively or treating the animal in a cruel manner, but the horse must know without a shadow of a doubt that this behavior will not be tolerated. As soon as the horse stops, the roof should fall in. I would immediately punish it by hitting it firmly behind my leg with a whip. Once the horse has been punished, forget the incident and ride to fence as though nothing had happened.

Ultimately, if you have a horse that is just belligerent or that you can't get to go forward to the jumps, you are in trouble. Under these circumstances, it may be best to get help or find yourself another horse.

A horse that gets faster while jumping a course can be unnerving to ride, especially for the novice. This type of horse often starts the course quietly but then gets stronger and stronger as it jumps more jumps. Anxiety may be at the bottom of this situation, whether it's the rider's tension or apprehension or the horse's trepidation about the jumps. The rider with this problem should analyze whether he or she gets anxious and increases the pace as the course goes on, or if the horse initiates the change of speed. In either circumstance, the problem can be helped greatly by mixing jumping and flatwork together. While you're doing a collected trot, jump a couple of fences. Then do another maneuver on the flat, such as the counter-canter or a flying change. After that, jump a few more obstacles. The idea is to teach the horse that jumping is merely a routine part of the flatwork it is doing. Ultimately, the horse should not differentiate going to the jumps from flatwork.

Mixing up the jumping and flatwork is also helpful with a horse that gets excited when it sees a jump. This type of horse, like the rushers, needs to experience jumping as part of a normal routine.

A sampling of gymnastic exercises

Virtually all horses, no matter what their problems, can benefit from gymnastic exercises. You can teach your horse to shorten its stride, to lengthen its stride, and many other useful skills with gymnastics. As with all training exercises, it is best to tailor gymnastics to suit your horse and to take your time in increasing the level of difficulty.

Once a horse beginning its jumper training is jumping crossrails, you can set a comfortable distance to a second jump that will be the out element of a one-stride in-and-out. You can start with a distance between the jumps of 18 to 20 feet, which allows you to trot over the crossrail and canter one stride to a second crossrail. The second crossrail can soon become a low vertical. As your horse's confidence and skills increase, you should raise the jumps and increase the distance between them appropriately. Once the horse is comfortably jumping the out element as a vertical, build it up into a small oxer. As your prospect gets comfortable with these changes, gradually increase the distance between the two fences until you have a normal 24- or 25-foot distance at which point you should be cantering through the exercise.

Figure 8 is an illustration of four types of gymnastic exercises you can try. Note that these exercises are not appropriate for a very green horse.

The obstacles in the first line are set so they can be jumped from either direction. Start with a vertical and measure 32 feet to an oxer. Measure 25 feet to another oxer and then 32 feet to a vertical. What this gives you is a very steady two strides to the first oxer, one quite long stride to another oxer and then two very quiet strides to the vertical. Again, this is not an easy exercise and should not be a gymnastic you would ride through very early in your training program; your first gymnastics should have perfect distances based on a 12-foot stride. Before attempting more demanding distance problems, like those in the diagram, your horse should be very comfortable jumping through gymnastics with normal distances. The jumps here can be about 3 feet in height and the oxers should be square. If your horse can jump square oxers, which are the most difficult, any other type will be easy.

The second line begins with a 26-foot distance between two verticals, which should be ridden in one very long stride. Next is a 32-foot distance to an oxer which is ridden in two quite short strides. Next is 53 feet to another oxer, and there are two ways to ride this. You can go from the left corner of the first oxer to the left corner of the second in three long strides, or from the right corner to the right corner in four steady strides.

On the third line, you start with an oxer and go 39 feet to a vertical, which is a long two strides. Next is a steady one stride in 21 feet to a vertical. Following that is a 39-foot distance to an oxer, to be ridden in a long two strides again. Here we are working on going from long to short to long again.

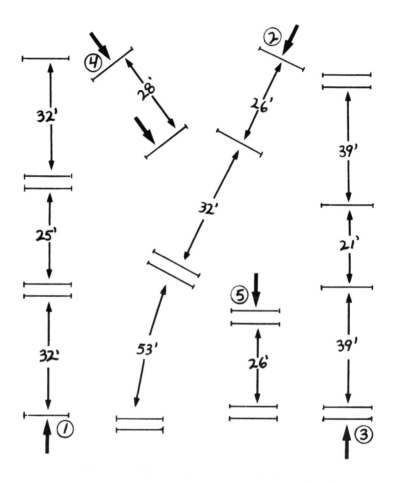

Figure 8. Four types of gymnastic exercises.

Line four starts with an option. You have two verticals, 29 feet apart. Your option is to ride the exercise in a very long one stride or a very steady two strides. If you are riding an inexperienced horse, you should add the stride and choose the steady option. I would concentrate on shortening first; it is much easier to work on lengthening the horse's stride later in its training. From there, I did not measure a distance to line five, which leads to two oxers, 26 feet apart. That is quite a long distance, especially since you probably will approach the oxers on a broken line. You can either leave out a stride or add one between lines four and five. If you leave out the stride, your horse will be moving forward with more momentum which will make it easier for you to cover 26 feet in one stride. To do this smoothly, make the decision to move forward early, not right in front of the jump. If you add the stride from line four to line five, making the 26 feet in one stride will be long. Again, if you choose to add the stride, do your shortening early, not close to the fence.

Another helpful type of gymnastic exercise is the bounce or no-stride combination. Before progressing to the bounces diagrammed in figure 9, start with two crossrails set up 10 to 11 feet apart so your horse jumps in and out without taking a stride between the two jumps. When your horse has mastered jumping these small fences, make the crossrails into 2-1/2-foot verticals. When the horse is comfortable with those, add a third fence, a low oxer, at the end of the line.

When that elementary line rides well, you can go on to the illustrated bounces. Although these gymnastics seem tough, most

Figure 9. Four exercises using the bounce or no-stride combination.

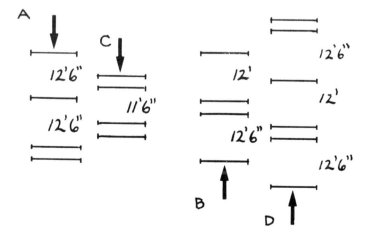

horses learn to go through them very quickly. These exercises do, however, get harder as you progress through them. Remember that it is very important to ride to bounces with a little pace. Do not slow the horse coming into a bounce. Instead, ask the horse to go forward.

Line A consists of a vertical to a vertical to an oxer. The 12-$^1/_2$-foot distance works wells for me. The fences do not have to be high. You can start at 2 feet, go to 2-$^1/_2$-feet, and then go up to 3 feet. The really good horses can jump the bounces much higher, but don't press it on your own. The oxer is an important element here because it makes the horse use its shoulders.

Line B goes from vertical to oxer to vertical. Notice that the last part is measured at only a 12-foot distance, rather than the previous 12-$^1/_2$-foot length. The reason for the decreased measurement is that the horse will land closer to the back rail of the middle element, and the center of its jumping arc will be the center of the oxer. As a result, you do not need quite as much room to jump out.

For line C, there are two oxers with the distance between measured at 11-$^1/_2$-feet. The space between two oxers is decreased because a horse takes off closer and lands closer to spreads. You always want to make the distance between two oxers in a bounce a little shorter so the horse does not have to take off too far away from the out element. To avoid getting in trouble, when setting up and practicing this line, do not make the jumps too high.

In line D, you go from a vertical to an oxer to another vertical and end with an oxer. The distances here are set at 12-$^1/_2$-feet, except between the first oxer and the second vertical, where the distance is decreased to 12 feet. The reason for the decrease, again, is because you are landing off an oxer. The final distance is 12-$^1/_2$-feet, which is designed to ask the horse to stretch just a little bit.

An advantage to using bounce gymnastics in your training program is that it is an excellent way to teach your horse to use its legs. When going through a bounce grid, the horse clears each fence by pulling its legs out of the way, not by jumping higher. Its torso should stay at the same height over each jump. If the body gets higher, the horse's jumping arc will get longer and it will run into the next jump. That is why if the horse jumps too big and gets high over the fence, it penalizes itself. Once they understand this, horses will pull their legs out of the way to avoid hitting the fences.

The distance measurements given here are not going to fit every horse. You may need to adjust these to make them suitable for your horse. For example, if you have a horse that is overjumping the first fence and keeps hitting the second jump, you need to give it more room. If you let the animal keep crashing into the obstacles, it may lose its desire to jump.

Don't try to set up this whole series and ride through it at once. Do a little bit at a time for the best results. Base your choice of gymnastics on how your horse is developing and what will help you solve your horse's problems.

When planning your gymnastic combinations, you should decide whether your horse hurries and needs work on quiet distances or if your horse is too sluggish and needs work on long distances. Remember, you will need to do both distances well, especially if you plan to move up the levels. There are all kinds of gymnastics you can make up on your own; the ones here are just several examples.

Should you give up or persevere?

When do you give up on a horse? I would give up on a horse that is becoming dangerous or so nervous it won't listen to my aids. When a rider's safety is at risk, I would suggest giving up. You also might want to give up with a horse that is a habitual stopper. Some riders have done very well with horses others have given up on, though. The story of Kathy Kusner and a horse named Aberali is a good example of this (see photograph). For Kathy, it paid to persevere. She bought Aberali from the

Kathy Kusner, who rode for the United States Equestrian Team, on Aberali, a horse she cured from stopping. Notice the use of a hackamore (a bridle with no bit). This picture was taken in Aachen, Germany, over the puissance wall.

Italian Equestrian Team many years ago. The horse was a notorious stopper. Kathy worked very hard to turn this horse around. She was very strict with him and made it clear that he had to obey her. Kathy went on to have great success with this horse in international competition. Others would have given up.

We had a mare named White Lightning that I might have given up on had she not been bred by Mary's mother and given to us. She had a difficult temperament and did not always use her legs well. Looking back, I'm glad we persevered with her. Both Mary and I had great success on this mare. Mary won a team silver medal on her in the 1967 Pan American Games in

Winnipeg, Canada, and competed with her in the 1968 Olympics. She also had a string of Nations Cup victories on her in 1968, including the classes in London, Dublin, New York, and Toronto. That year, Mary also won the Queen Elizabeth II Cup in London on her. In 1972, I rode White Lightning to a team silver medal in the Olympics.

Finding professional help

With jumping courses getting more and more technical, many riders seek professional help to improve themselves, their horses,

Mary Chapot on White Lightning. Bred by Mary's mother, White Lightning was a difficult mare at first, but went on to win numerous classes in the late sixties, including Nations Cup victories in London, Dublin, New York, and Toronto. White Lightning competed in two Olympic Games: the 1968 games in Mexico, with Mary Chapot, and the 1972 games in Munich, with Frank Chapot, where they won the team silver medal.

Mary Chapot using a lead pad on White Lightning. Mary had to carry so much lead to make 165 pounds that she used to put some in stitched pockets in the girth so as not to have all the weight under her legs. Note the use of a sheepskin girth cover to protect the horse, and a breastplate and overgirth to hold the girth in place. Kathy Kusner, who was even lighter than Mary, had mercury inserts put in the seat of her saddle. It was a wonderful solution until the insert broke open once!

and their competitive edge. You should choose a professional carefully. Find one whose methods suit your personality and whose background is compatible with your riding goals.

First, you should know yourself. Do you need an instructor who is very strict and will motivate you by scolding you? Or would you benefit more from someone who is more sympathetic and reassuring? Certainly, you want someone who will bring out the best in you. You also might want to keep in mind that this is a recreational sport that should be enjoyable. You may not want to train with someone whose lesson style you would find unpleasant.

I also would not base my selection of an instructor solely on a person's reputation. The professional with the big reputation may not be right for you. There are other factors I would weigh when making a choice. I would watch prospective instructors. See how they communicate with their students and observe how the horses they train perform. An instructor's success as a rider and trainer should be a definite consideration. If a professional is successful with others, he or she may not be successful with you, but it certainly increases the odds in your favor. It is also wise to choose someone who can help you achieve your goals, whether your goals are to qualify for an adult or children's jumper championship or to try out for the United States Equestrian Team.

6

On course

*W*ithout a doubt, the most popular classes at horse shows are those with the lowest fences, and I suspect that this will always be the case. However, the entire jumper division has grown dramatically in recent years. Even entries in the classes with higher fences have more than doubled in the last decade. For horses and riders who are more comfortable jumping lower fences, there is now the tremendously popular children's/adult division, along with schooling jumpers. From there, horses can progress through the preliminary division right up the ladder to grand prix, if they have the ability. Riders can progress as well through the junior or amateur-owner classes into the open divisions, if they wish. However, just as there is a world of difference between the curricula in grammar school and in graduate school, there is a big difference in the skill level needed to jump a schooling jumper course and a grand prix course. In this chapter, I will walk an amateur-owner jumper course and a grand prix course with you. I will also suggest many options you and your horse can try and some pointers to help you win at these levels.

An amateur-owner course

Let's begin by walking an amateur-owner jumper course. I have taken the schooling jumper course from Chapter 4, shifted some fences slightly, and added a few more obstacles. The addition of just a few more fences makes a far more complicated course, especially if the ring is small (see figure 10).

Fences 1, 2, and 3 are set in a broken line. This may give you some options, depending upon the size of the ring. In a large ring you will have more strides between each fence and, therefore, more options than you would in a small ring. When you walk this line, bear in mind the length of your horse's stride, and whether it is apt to jump toward the left or right over the fence. Plan to ride this line in a manner that best suits your horse.

After fence 3 comes a fence on the turn. This jump may come up very quickly, especially if the ring is small. Although I don't usually walk off distances around a corner, in a tight ring I would, because there could be a related distance between fences 3 and 4. In a large, open field, I would rely on my eye and jump fence 4 as a single obstacle, possibly shaving a tiny bit off the turn, if the time allowed is tight.

The double combination from the schooling jumper class has now become a triple, and, again, depending on the size of the ring, may not give you much time to get organized. Because the first fence of the combination is an oxer, treat it with respect and prepare your horse on the turn by increasing its impulsion, but not necessarily its speed. You won't know until you walk the

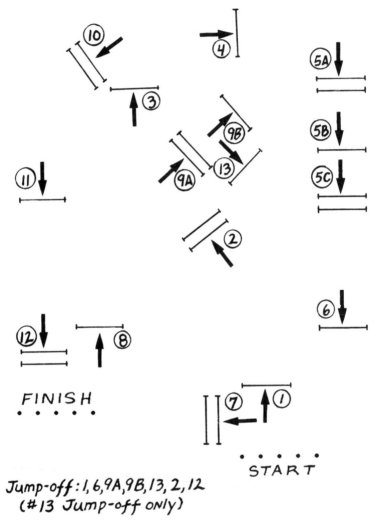

Jump-off: 1, 6, 9A, 9B, 13, 2, 12
(#13 Jump-off only)

Figure 10. An amateur-owner jumper course.

course whether the course designer has created any distance problems for you within the combination. However, whether the distance inside is long or tight, if you overdo your preparation and jump into the line with too much or too little impulsion, you will risk having faults at one or more elements.

Fence 6 is in a straight line after the triple combination, and it surely will be a related distance. Keep in mind when you walk the course that you will be riding to this obstacle after landing off fence 5C, an oxer. When jumping an oxer, the center of your horse's arc will be over the middle of the spread, and the horse will land closer to the back rail than if that fence had been a vertical. If you forget this, you may be surprised to find the distance to fence 6 riding longer than you expected.

On the course diagram, it looks as though fence 7, an oxer, will come up fairly quickly. Yet this may not be the case when the jumps are actually set up in the ring. For our purposes though, let's assume that it is close to the turn and be careful not to lose impulsion or concentration here.

So far, we have had several jumps in quick succession. If you have had a rail down or made a mistake, this is not the time to dwell on it. What's done is done. Concentrate instead on what is coming up next.

Fence 8 is a vertical followed by a broken line to the double combination, 9A and 9B. Approaching fence 8, you may need to steady your horse and balance it again after the oxer on the turn, especially if you had to create a lot of energy to jump the spread. How you ride the broken line will depend somewhat on the distance within the in-and-out, as well as the length of your horse's stride. As in the first line of the course between fences 1, 2, and 3, be aware of your options and ride this line to suit your horse. Whatever plan you choose, make your adjustments early and smoothly, not at the last minute.

From the course diagram, it looks difficult to go inside fence 4 to get to number 10. However, when you walk the course, take a look at this turn in case you need to shave a few seconds to be within the time allowed.

From fence 10 to 11, you have another broken line, this time curved to the left. I would expect fences 11 and 12 to be the largest on the course and to have a related distance between them. The distance between 11 and 12 will have a direct bearing on how you ride the broken line between 10 and 11. A long distance between the last two fences may prompt you to ride directly and aggressively, while a tight distance may ask you to swing wide and add a stride. I think the hardest problem to solve is a tight distance to a wide oxer. This is a real test of scope, so if this is the case to the last fence, don't lose your concentration here.

The finish line on this course is straight ahead, so getting there won't be a problem. When walking a course, notice where the start and finish markers are. Sometimes due to limited equipment or lack of space, they can end up in an unusual place, and you will feel pretty silly gaining faults or being eliminated for missing the start or finish.

When you walk the course, don't forget to walk the jump-off course. Sometimes a turn that looks entirely possible from the ground doesn't work out very well when you are actually riding it. You may even want to ride by a particularly difficult turn when you are making your preliminary circle so you can see if the turn looks as promising from your horse's back as it did from the ground. Whatever plan you devise, you will have a much better chance for success if your decisions are made by walking the jump-off course, rather than by watching at the back gate while someone else rides it.

If you are trying to win this class, go through the start in the jump-off the same way you plan to go through the finish—fast. On this jump-off course, your turn to the second fence, 6, is well beyond fence 1. Therefore, you don't need to worry about "killing your turn" (having your momentum carry you beyond where you meant to turn) by jumping the first fence with too much pace. Jump fence 1 with as much speed as you can handle. Keep your eye on fence 6 and turn back to it just as close as you can. It's a vertical, so you don't have to worry about clearing a spread.

From fence 6, you will be turning right back to 9A and 9B, the double combination. The FEI requires combinations in the jump-off, and you will find a lot of basic jump-off courses will also have them. A combination in the jump-off requires an accurate ride and forces most riders to slow down a little bit.

I hope you will be able to turn inside fence 1 to get to 9A and 9B. You will be risking knocking down fence 6 with your horse's hind legs by starting this sharp turn in the air, but you often have to take a chance to win. Remember to push the horse around the turn rather than pull, as I described in Chapter 3. And use finesse when turning, don't just yank hard on your horse's mouth over the top of the fence.

You will approach 9A at an angle. Remember to keep steering as you jump into the combination so you don't run by 9B on the left side. After the double, you must make a left turn to fence 13, a jump that was not in the first round. If you made a good turn to the in-and-out, you probably jumped 9B on the left side, automatically setting up a good turn to fence 13. From the course chart, it looks easy to turn inside fence 4, but jumps do not always end up in the ring exactly as they are on the diagram. This is a turn you definitely want to look at when you walk the course, because if you have to go around fence 4, you should not be so anxious to jump 9B in the left corner.

Adding a fence in the jump-off is permissible, and many course designers do this. The new fence will be marked on the chart as "jump-off only" or with an X, such as 13X. Obviously, it is a fence you did not jump in the first round, so, you must hope that it will not spook your horse when you are trying to go fast. Oddly enough, some horses lose their concentration when asked to jump from between two barriers, be it a large hedge, or in this case, 9A and 9B. Make sure your horse is focused on the jump and not on what's beside it.

After fence 13, you must roll back to fence 2, which is an oxer. This is a difficult challenge as you must maintain enough impulsion through this very sharp turn to jump the spread. If this is a class where the jump-off takes place after all the entrants have jumped the first round, the course designer may lower or narrow the fence a bit to tempt you to take a chance here, which also makes the class more exciting for the spectators. If you are planning to jump fence 2 on an angle, starting to turn for fence 12, remember you will be jumping a wider spread and be sure you have enough horse under you to clear it. If the fence has remained or become high and square, treat it with respect because you will be coming off a sharp turn. This may not be the place to become a hero. Try to see what the course designer does to the fences between rounds, or have someone watch for you if you can't be there. Even something that seems minor, like changing the depth of a jump cup, can make a major difference.

Depending on the size of the ring, you could have a bit of a gallop to fence 12, the last jump. Be careful, however, not to let your horse get flat, or it may knock down the front rail of the oxer. If you are late in the jump-off, you will have some idea of how much of a chance to take, but if you are early in the jumping order, you will have to take your best shot. In any case, make the turn after fence 2 before you start a mad gallop. Simply kicking your horse as soon as you land will carry you wide and waste time, even though you may think you are flying.

Continue straight through the finish and don't slow down until you are absolutely sure you are through the timers. Sometimes if the timers are set at an angle you can save time by turning slightly after the last fence. On this course, however, the timers are straight ahead.

If this class requires the rider to stay in the ring and jump off right away, your strategy would be different. In that type of class, after crossing the finish line of the course, you have sixty seconds after the bell rings to start the jump-off. Use those sixty seconds productively. Don't just wander around the ring. Instead, do some turns on the haunches and rein-backs and whatever else you need to do to get your horse prepared to make some sharp turns, be quick, and perform the maneuvers you'll be wanting in the jump-off. Gauge your sixty seconds. It's a long time to get your horse settled, relaxed, obedient, and listening to your aids. Whatever you do, don't wander through the starting line in the direction of the first fence. If the judge is on the ball he or she will have the timers activated and you will be penalized three jumping faults and possibly earn some time faults as well.

At this level, the horse should be comfortable jumping over a variety of obstacles. For example, if this were a major show, the course designer could put in a liverpool, which is water under a jump. If the course designer made the second fence a liverpool, you are being tested. You will not get very good grades on the test if you have to resort to spurs and a stick to get over it. If you have a big problem with the liverpool, you may have to change your plan for fence 3. Hopefully, this is a big ring and you will have some options. If not, do the best you can as the next fences come up quickly. If you and your horse are agitated after the liverpool, it will be hard to salvage much of the round.

A grand prix course

A grand prix class is the most difficult jumping test a horse and rider can encounter in the show ring. If the amateur-owner jumper course we just talked about can be thought of as an upper-level test of the rider's skill, and the horse's scope and adjustability, this grand prix course can be thought of as the final exam. Most of the questions asked by the course designer on this test will be at a very high degree of difficulty.

Using the course diagram in figure 11, let's take a look at a grand prix course. This course will be jumped in a large, outdoor field. As we proceed, remember that quite a bit of thought has to be given to every part of the course. The starting marker is at a slight angle. If completing the course in the time allowed is on your mind (and it probably should be), you may want to begin on the left side of the marker. You will definitely want to do so in the jump-off.

The first fence is an inviting one. Not all course designers give you a relatively easy first fence (Bert deNemethy never does). Rather than think of this jump as a given, think of it as preparation for what is coming up next. The following line is very difficult. You will be jumping fence 2, a vertical, into a line with water.

This line will have related distances with enough room for options. The course designer is asking you to jump the water

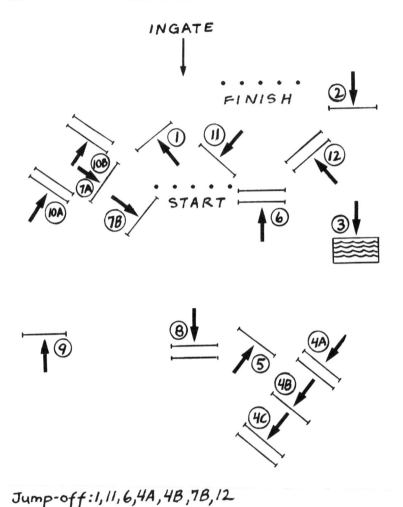

Jump-off: 1, 11, 6, 4A, 4B, 7B, 12

Figure 11. A grand prix course.

very early on course. This is a test of your horse's training and temperament. Most horses will generate their own impulsion as a course goes along, and you will often finish the course with a lot more horse under you than when you started. On this particular course, with the water jump so early, you are going to have to generate a great deal of energy for your horse to jump this wide spread, and you run the risk of having a very excited horse as you approach the triple combination. If your horse is a very good water jumper, you might exercise your option here of adding a stride to the water, leaving you with a more relaxed horse afterwards. However, if you use this option, make your adjustment early so that you aren't slowing your horse down right in front of the water. If your horse is a more casual water jumper, you had better keep galloping here, leaving out the stride so that you meet the water going forward.

San Lucas was one of the best water jumpers I have ever ridden. He was very careful and had such a long stride that I had to do very little to increase his stride to a big water jump. This gave me a great edge in big grand prix and Olympic courses. Because there was little we had to do before the jump, San Lucas remained calm afterwards.

Frank Chapot and San Lucas jumping a water jump. "San Lucas was one of the best water jumpers I have ever ridden. He was very careful and had such a long stride that I had to do very little to increase his stride to a big water jump."

After the water jump, the distance to the triple combination walks in five strides in a direct line. Because of the momentum you had to create to get over the water, this line will ride very tight if you ride straight to the combination. Instead, bow out a little to the left, giving yourself more room to use up your horse's lengthened stride after the water. The question is how far to come out. I can't place a marker on the ground and tell you, if you go around this, the distance will work out perfectly. Here is where your knowledge of your horse's stride and your ability to make smooth, quick adjustments, come into play. The fact that 4A is an oxer doesn't allow much room for error or nervous, abrupt adjustments.

This combination walks in a normal one stride to one stride. However, if you are still carrying a lot of extra energy as you jump in, the horse's momentum will carry you too close to 4B, forcing a bit of an awkward jump here, and then 4C will not ride as easily as it walked. The course designer did not have to build this line very high to create a difficult test. Instead he has used some flat cups to hold the rails. It will be easy to incur a fault here.

Following 4A, 4B, and 4C, you have a sharp turn to fence 5. Use this time to reorganize if necessary, but don't wander all over the ring to get to the next jump. This is a perfect opportunity to save some ground if the time allowed is tight. The distance between fences 5 and 6 is related and can be bent to accommodate your horse's length of stride.

Next, you have quite a long way to go to 7A and 7B, a pair of verticals set at a tight distance. Don't let your horse lose its concentration as he goes by the in-gate at this end of the ring. Even though this combination is tight, don't start setting up for it immediately after 6. You will waste time riding the turn at a slow canter. Instead, simply let your horse gallop around the turn in a relaxed, balanced manner. (I do realize that this is not always possible, but it is the ideal you want.) As you make your turn to the combination, slow up a little in anticipation of the tight distance inside.

Fence 8 is quite big and wide. Again we have a broken line as an approach, so you can make use of the various options to suit your horse, but don't underestimate the width of this fence.

From fence 8, you have a comfortable turn to 9. I have no special advice here, except again, to avoid wasting time. Fence 9 is quite a tall vertical followed by an oxer combination with a long distance inside. With the broken line from 9 to 10A and 10B, you can afford to ride the vertical carefully and use an option to the combination. However, even though this set of fences is headed toward the in-gate, treat them with respect and, as you plan your option in the bent line, leave yourself some room to drive.

Fence 11 requires a sharp turn back from the in-gate after a big, forward effort. Don't lose concentration here; your horse may be tired and think it is finished.

Fence 12 is very big and square off another turn, past the water. Keep your impulsion up around the turn so that you have plenty of horse to jump the spread. Don't let your horse get its eye on the water and spook away from it. This would make an already short turn a lot more difficult.

Your finish line is on a slight angle, with the shortest route from the last jump on the right side. Make sure you take advantage of that route, especially if you are worried about the time allowed.

The jump-off is quite straightforward. Approach fence 1 from the left corner of the starting line. This is not only the shortest route through the start to the first fence, but it sets up your turn to fence 11. Make the best turn you can back to 11, then gallop up to your rollback to fence 6. You may have to give this turn a little room, depending on the size of the oxer. Ideally, after fence 6, you would like to turn right inside both fence 12 and fence 3, the water, to get to 4A and 4B. It is impossible to tell if you can do this by looking at the course chart. You need to walk the route and consider your strategy, based on how your horse goes. Riding 4A and 4B will depend on what adjustments the course designer has made, and where you turn and make your approach. 4C will have been removed, leaving you with a long gallop and quick turn back inside 10A and 10B to 7B. (7A will be removed.) Don't waste time setting up your turn midway down the field. Get to the spot, then fix it. From the course chart, it looks as if you have an easy turn inside the water to fence 12 and a direct line to the right side of the finish. Walk this route though, and make sure it is really there.

Expanding your jump inventory

I said earlier that you do not have to have a grand prix course in your backyard to teach your horse jumping fundamentals. If you are on a budget, you don't have to spend a lot of money on your practice jumps. Get what you can afford. However, certain types of obstacles would be very useful in your schooling ring, especially if you are working with a green horse. Most inexperienced horses spook at a rolltop, perhaps because of the way it reflects the light. If you can, buy one—even a used one is a good addition to your ring. With a hammer, nails, a heavy sheet of plywood and some paint, you can make the backside of your rolltop look like a wall and give your horse some practice over two different types of solid fences. Otherwise, obstacles such as a wall can be found at most shows and easily schooled over in a low hunter class.

An important addition, once your horse has mastered the basics, is some type of artificial liverpool or water jump. You find more and more of these obstacles on courses at all sorts of shows. The first time most horses see a water jump, they are not very happy to jump it. There are several kinds you can buy, made of plastic, canvas, or rubber. Or, you can make your own with blue canvas and a little wooden frame to put around it. At the shows, many people bring their blue strips of canvas to use in the schooling area.

Artificial flowers in boxes would be a useful but expensive addition for your practice area, as these are commonly used to decorate the jumps at most shows. However, if you are in the right place at the right time for the sales, and if you don't mind the bunch with one flower missing that no one else wants, you can make your course look quite impressive. Otherwise, as with the wall, your horse can learn as much, if not more, about jumping different obstacles at shows as it could at home.

More training hints

As the jumps get bigger, you should not have to change your approach much at all. You might, however, need to generate more impulsion as the oxers get wider. This is where your basic flatwork should help you. Ideally, you should be able to create enough energy to jump the spreads without turning your horse into a maniac.

When you are riding to a big, square oxer, you want to take off closer to the jump than you would to a vertical. The theory here is that the farther you leave the ground from a spread fence, the farther your horse will have to jump to clear the back rail. You will also land closer to an oxer than to a vertical, which is an important detail to keep in mind when walking a course.

When schooling at home, use mostly square oxers, rather than sloping "ramps." Your horse should rapidly learn to be quick with its knees leaving the ground and to respect the front rail. If you can jump square oxers well, you will be able to jump all the other spread configurations easily, including ascending oxers, triple bars, and hogs-backs. Another type of spread I school my horses over at home is a Swedish oxer. These oxers tend to look a little spooky to a young horse and may cause it to drift to one corner or the other. When riding to this type of jump, you need to keep your horse in the center to avoid a rail down. I don't school much over ramp-type spreads at home unless a horse has a confidence problem.

When schooling at home, incorporate some lines where you can jump a tight distance to a wide oxer. It is relatively easy to

Good Twist trying very hard over a Swedish oxer at the Piping Rock Horse Show in Locust Valley, Long Island, in 1965. The Irish often refer to this type of jump as a "drunken parallel." Today, for safety, we do not build this type of oxer with so many rails on the back. One rail or two at the most is sufficient. (Photo by Budd)

jump an oxer by itself. You will find it is also not too hard to jump a vertical to an oxer with a distance of 50 feet in between in three strides. However, decrease the distance to 45 feet, then start to spread the oxer, and you have a very hard test indeed. There is no room inside to drive at the oxer (unless you trot to the line), so you cannot solve the problem with speed. This is where you need more impulsion; you need to get your horse's rpms near the red line but keep its transmission in a low gear. It is very difficult, especially for a novice rider, to sit quietly when asking the horse to jump wide.

Inexperienced horses often try to get high instead of wide over spread jumps and may very well come down on the back rail. When Gem Twist was young and green, he wanted to jump everything too high. We worried about how he would jump the very wide oxers he would face in the future. To improve his style, we schooled him over low, but very wide spreads with different approach distances, some long, others tight. He learned

Good News Joe over a Swedish oxer at the Children's Services Horse Show in Farmington, Connecticut, in the early 1970s. You can see he has the same instinct not to hit jumps as his father, Good Twist, both horses clearing the jump with ample room to spare. Again, I don't like to see so many rails on the back of an oxer. Note, too, the square rails in very deep cups. I'm not going to have a rail down here without knocking over the entire standard. This is thankfully not an issue today, with our wide selection of jump cups and rounded rails. (Photo by Tarrance Photos)

to use his natural ability to the utmost, although he will still jump extraordinarily high on occasion.

Natural obstacles

Natural obstacles such as banks, grobs, and ditches are rarely seen in this country but are often jumped in Europe. If you are in a special competition, such as a derby, you can count on having these types of fences included in the course. Several permanent show grounds with large enough rings recently have added a bank or a ditch, and I think we will see more in the future. The course designer has to be protective of the footing around these permanent jumps, but I like to use them in my courses as they add a degree of difficulty (until the horses and riders get used to them).

Most horses master banks quite quickly. Once they get the idea of unfolding their legs to land on top, they can handle most presentations easily. Jumping off a bank is often more of a problem for the rider than for the horse. From a horse's back, the way down looks very long. Ride to a bank aggressively. This is one jump you can't knock down. A good, solid ride will get your horse well up on top, while a halfhearted effort by horse and rider can only lead to problems. You certainly don't want to come barreling off the bank with the same zeal you had jumping up, but in most cases this won't be a concern. A horse's natural caution will slow him down once he gets on top of the bank. You may encounter a fence on top or one at the bottom just after you jump down. You want to give your horse a chance to think and figure things out for itself as there won't be much time for you to do it all for the horse. Remember to steer. Many horses will be surprised the first time they jump up on a bank and some will try to wheel around or dart off to the side. As you approach and jump a bank, sit up straighter than you normally would and position your leg a little in front of you. This is one time you don't want to wind up on the horse's neck if it makes a mistake.

The bank at the USET training center in Gladstone, New Jersey. (Photo by Mary Chapot)

A rider jumping up on a low schooling bank. She is riding aggressively, the only way to ride a young horse over a bank so the horse has the impulsion to get on top. The bank may only be 3 feet high, but the horse must jump higher to get its whole body on top of the bank. (Photo by Mary Chapot)

Rider coming off the bank with just a placed takeoff rail on the bank. Notice that the rider has her leg forward and is in the "safety seat" in case the horse stumbles when it lands. (Photo by Jackie Promaulayko)

Most horses are not enthusiastic when first asked to negotiate ditches and grobs. The best solution, if you are going to enter competitions that have these types of obstacles, is to go to a place where you can school over them. Young horses and many older ones tend to think that open, dry ditches are very spooky. They look down into the hole or ditch as they approach it, and the closer they get, the more uninviting it becomes. Horses can get so fascinated with the ditch that sometimes they forget about any fence that might be set over it or behind it. The result is often a rail down, if they jump the obstacle at all. My advice here is to ride aggressively and try not to have the first ditch you ever jump be in the show ring. If you have to dig one yourself, do so. It doesn't have to be very deep or very wide to work well for practice.

A grob, which is sometimes called a sunken road, compounds the ditch problem by its configuration. The ditch itself is located

A more difficult test. This horse is coming off the bank with a rail set higher than the bank and beyond it. (Photo by Jackie Promaulayko)

A moment later, rider showing the "safety seat" but not interfering with the horse's mouth. (Photo by Jackie Promaulayko)

A relaxed, confident horse jumping a small obstacle on top of a bank. A pretty picture for an equitation class, but I would prefer the rider's leg to be farther forward. (Photo by Mary Chapot)

This rider is doing the wrong thing, being too far forward. If the horse stops or stumbles, the rider may fall off. (Photo by Mary Chapot)

at the bottom of a slope, followed by an incline, with the natural boundary left over from the excavation on either side. Most horses are reluctant to even go down into this obstacle, much less over the ditch at the bottom. The most challenging setup of a grob is when it includes a rather open vertical at the top, followed by one or two strides down to the ditch with an oxer built over it, followed by one or two strides up the hill to another vertical. I would recommend patience and plenty of time to get your horse used to these jumps. Most horses are very reluctant when they first encounter them.

It is not uncommon to find a water jump on upper-level courses. Once your horse has mastered the water jump and tries hard over it, don't keep practicing. If your horse finds out that it really does not hurt to step on the tape or the edge of the water jump, it can get very casual about clearing the jump. This is one instance where too much practice will not make perfect. (For information on training horses to jump water, see Chapter 8.)

The grob at the USET training center in Gladstone, New Jersey. (Photo by Mary Chapot)

On course, you should ride to all these natural obstacles in an aggressive manner. I would especially advise this when approaching a bank to help your horse jump up onto it. If you are timid in your ride, your horse might agree with you and stop. If you are quite sure your horse won't balk at these obstacles, you can relax a bit and ride in your usual manner. However, when jumping these or anything else unusual, the best maxim is, when in doubt, go forward.

Weather and terrain

All outdoor shows are affected at one time or another by weather. A long, dry spell can mean hard ground, while prolonged rain brings on mud and deep or slippery footing. When the ground is hard, I often cut back on the number of classes I enter. Even if a horse is young and perfectly sound, constant pounding on hard ground can ultimately take its toll.

There is a certain amount of judgment involved with showing in the rain. So-called all-weather surfaces are close to ideal because they are nearly the same, wet or dry. Many horse shows have at least one ring of this sort. The type of surface that poses the greatest problem in the rain is the beautiful grass field. Often, if the rain occurs at the beginning of the show, the management is able to cancel or shift classes to save the field for the big classes at the end of the week. However, if it rains on grand prix day, you're pretty much stuck. If your horse doesn't handle uncertain footing well, panics when it slips, or has a soundness problem that deep footing might aggravate, you may want to consider scratching. However, most horses can handle a wide variety of slippery footing by using studs in their shoes. When jumping on a grass field, you will need studs to give you more traction, whether the surface is wet or dry.

There are almost as many different types of studs as there are horses. Everyone has favorites. If you have never used studs before, your local tack shop or your farrier can probably offer some advice on what you will need for various surfaces. I prefer to use the smallest studs available that still maintain traction. The wetter the surface, the larger the stud you will need. However, I don't like to use the really big ones on the inside of the foot, especially on the back feet, in case the horse should step on itself. I prefer a big stud on the outside heel and a smaller one on the inside, footing permitting.

It takes some horses time to get used to studs. When the horse moves without studs, its foot slides a little bit as it hits the ground. However, when a horse is wearing studs, this little bit of give is eliminated, and the whole leg gets more of a shock as the foot lands on the ground. For this reason, I only use studs when the horse is jumping and the ground conditions demand them. If feasible, I have them removed as soon as the horse is finished. I hate to see horses standing on studs in the van or in a stall.

A course will ride differently if the footing is deep or wet than if it is dry. Distances will ride a little longer and jumps will ride a little higher. The easy three-stride distance you rode in the morning on dry ground may seem quite long later in the afternoon after a rainstorm when the track has been torn up by the hooves of other horses that have been on the course. To compensate for deep or slippery footing problems, you will be safest overriding your horse a bit. Have plenty of horse under you, as it will need extra impulsion to clear the fences. Don't be afraid to ride forward in adverse conditions. Underriding to the fences in the mud will get you in a lot more trouble than will overdoing it a little.

Even when a show is indoors, you can't count on perfect footing. You may need studs to help with traction here as well. Just because the show is indoors, don't leave the studs at home.

While some horses are very comfortable jumping on grass, others go best on sand. Hopefully, your horse will be happy on both, as you will certainly encounter all kinds of footing throughout your horse's career.

Besides noticing the ring surface, you also should be aware of the slope of the ground as you walk the course. Outdoor shows in the mountains can offer an added dimension to how you ride the course. Even a ring set on fairly flat land can have enough of a slope to make a difference in how a line rides. A tight distance set downhill will ride even tighter than it walks, and a long distance set going uphill can be a real challenge. As always, make your adjustments early. Do not wait for the last stride or two to increase or decrease your pace.

Poling—a fact of life in the jumper ring

Poling has generated a lot of controversy in Europe. It is against FEI rules, and in 1990, allegations about poling used as a training method by German rider Paul Schockemöhle caused a scandal that was ultimately resolved in his favor.

In America, poling is considered a legitimate training method that is permitted by the American Horse Shows Association when done with a taped bamboo pole, two inches or less in diameter. Poling is used to encourage a horse to jump cleanly. One year, we did not allow poling in this country and I've never seen horses so abused. Riders were pulling horses down over oxers, purposely misjudging distances, and jumping them over uninviting fences that were too high for their abilities, such as airy verticals 6 feet tall. These practices are far worse than poling because the rider is lying to his horse and taking the horse's confidence away. I believe the worst thing you can do to a horse is lie to it. Eventually the horse will lose its trust in you and will stop at the jumps.

The idea of setting a bamboo pole in front of an obstacle for a horse to hit when it jumps may seem harsh. However, when a bamboo offset is used properly, it is probably the most humane way to teach a careless horse not to hit the jumps.

When done properly, poling does make a horse jump higher and more carefully. Years ago, when most of the jumper classes were judged on touches, there were more poling experts be-

This is the wrong way to pole a horse. You want the horse to believe it has struck the rail of a jump when it hits the bamboo. With the technique shown here, the animal relates being hit with the pole with being hit by a longe whip, not the rail. (Photo by Jackie Promaulayko)

This is the correct way to sharpen a dull horse that is hitting the jumps. The animal does not see the bamboo and thinks, when the pole is raised to hit the horse's legs, that it has hit the rail rather than the bamboo pole. I always pole a horse over a low jump that does not require the horse to exert much effort. (Photo by Jackie Promaulayko)

Here is an example of a bamboo offset. The bamboo pole has been set in front of and slightly higher than the rails. This has created a false ground line, which is hard for the horse to judge. If the horse rubs the bamboo pole, the horse thinks it must try harder to clear the obstacle. To get the desired effect, the fence should be jumped towards the house in the background. Note that the ground line on the right side of the fence has been placed behind the vertical plane of the fence. This is not legal at shows. The ground line must be in the same vertical plane or in front of the fence. (Photo by Jackie Promaulayko)

cause it was used as a routine training method. Now, many people do it, but they pole their horses incorrectly because they have not been exposed to appropriate methods. The correct way to pole a horse is to use a light, taped, bamboo pole that is held parallel to the top rail of the fence and raised to tap the horse's legs lightly as it jumps. Another method is to use an offset bamboo pole that is not held by anyone (see photos). The offset consists of a bamboo pole set in front of the top rail, and maybe a little bit higher. Because the pole is placed in front of the fence's vertical plane, it is hard for a horse to judge the proper takeoff spot. When the horse approaches the obstacle, it does not see the pole and usually hits it with its legs as it jumps.

When that happens, the horse thinks it struck the rail of the fence. It hears a noise from striking the pole and its legs may feel slightly stung from the impact. Next time, the horse will try to jump higher to avoid that impact, thinking it misjudged the height of the fence. The impact of hitting a light bamboo pole is far less severe than the jolt of hitting a four-inch, solid wood rail.

If a horse is poled too often manually, it may become suspicious whenever it sees someone standing next to an obstacle. To avoid this predicament, use caution and moderation when poling.   I often see people pole horses by holding the pole away from the jump and swinging it like a baseball bat at the horse as it jumps. This is a very poor method for the simple reason that the horse will not associate the tap from the bamboo pole with hitting the fence. It makes the horse afraid of the trainer, instead of the jump, and you want the horse to respect the fence. The horse gets the feeling it is being hit with a whip. If you hit a horse with a longe whip, it runs away.   What does the horse learn from this experience? The horse learns to try to avoid the person, rather than the rail.

No matter what the rules about poling are, I think trainers will continue to use this training method, even if they have to be secretive about it. As long as poling is done correctly and in moderation, I don't think it is the worst way to teach a horse to jump cleanly. Of course, this method should not be used indiscriminately. If I am training a horse that is already careful, the last thing I would want to do is pole it and add more chicken to the training recipe. I would be concerned that the horse would then be more reluctant to jump and might stop more often. For example, I have never poled Gem Twist. Because he is already very careful, there is no valid reason to do so.

I would be in favor of changing the international rules to allow poling, particularly the bamboo offset. This method is not cruel. It hurts less for the horse to hit bamboo than the solid wood rail of a jump. I think if the rules were changed to allow the use of the offset, you would not have as many people poling behind the barn. I worry about how these people do their poling and what materials they use for their poles. They may be using a pole more severe than one of light bamboo.

After the controversy when Schockemöhle was accused of poling horses, a study was done in Germany about the effects of the practice. The study found that the force of a horse striking a bamboo pole was less harmful than striking the sort of wooden rail we use in the show ring. So, I think if we can avoid having the horse hit the show ring rail, it is better for both horse and rider.

7

Riding for the Team

If showing at the grand prix level is like climbing to the top of a mountain, riding for the United States Equestrian Team in international competition is like reaching the very top pinnacle of that mountain. I feel very lucky to have had this privilege, and I view my continued association with the Team as chef d'équipe as a great honor. I don't consider myself to be an emotional person, but I can't think of anything more thrilling than standing in an international arena and hearing our national anthem played.

With that great honor comes a great responsibility. When you ride for the USET, you are not just Frank Chapot, riding for yourself. You are representing your country, and the eyes of the

Olympic veteran Michael Matz blazing against the clock on Heisman, his 1992 Olympic mount. Without stopping the horse's forward motion, Matz starts his turn to the next jump while landing off this one. Notice that he is pushing his horse through the turn, not pulling it. (Photo © Cathrin Cammett)

world are on you. At least that is how it seems to me. Some riders cope well with the pressure. Others don't. There have been a lot of very good riders with good horses who did not perform as well when they rode with the flag on their saddle pads as without. Riding for the Team can bring out the best in people, but it can also bring out the worst.

I certainly experienced that feeling of pressure when I rode for the Team, even when I had been riding internationally for years. The first class I rode in at an international show always made me

British Equestrian Team rider John Whitaker on Milton. Milton was named the second best horse in the world after Gem Twist at the 1990 World Championships in Stockholm. Here, this great duo is seen clearing a jump in that competition. (Photo copyright © Tish Quirk)

*Two views of Gem Twist, showing the great athletic ability that earned
him two silver medals. Here he is ridden by Greg Best at the 1988
Olympics. (Photo copyright © Tish Quirk)*

a little breathless. I felt that way, no matter how fit I was. I'm
sure my anxiety was the cause. When I went into the ring, I
didn't want anyone to watch me ride and say, "Why did they let
him ride for the Team?" I also did not want to be the one to let
my teammates down or have my mistake ruin the Team's chances
of victory. When I first started riding in Nations Cups, this
particular pressure was compounded because only three Team
members were allowed to ride. All three scores counted. I certainly did not want to be the rider who let the Team down.

I remember the 1960 Olympic Games in Rome, when we still
competed under these rules. The first British rider went in the
stadium and was eliminated. After that, the British Team mem-

Here, Gem Twist and Greg Best at The Washington International Horse Show, 1987. (Photo by Pennington Galleries.)

bers packed their bags and went home. They did not have a chance of winning a medal so there was no reason for the others to ride. In recent years, this pressure has been somewhat reduced: Now, four riders compete in the Nations Cups and the three best scores are used for the final tally.

Of course, the ultimate international contest is the Olympics. There is only one Olympic competition every four years and only four riders can be chosen. Of all the riders chosen throughout the world, only three teams and three individuals come home with medals. So, the stature of competing at the Olympics makes the pressure quite intense.

Here is Lisa Jacquin, a member of the 1988 silver-medal U.S. Team, at the Seoul Olympics on her Thoroughbred partner For The Moment. The pair was also selected for the 1992 Olympic Team, with For The Moment, at age eighteen, the oldest horse on the Team. (Photo copyright © Tish Quirk)

Having ridden in six Olympics and ninety-eight Nations Cups, I understand very well the pressures and responsibilities that come with riding for the Team. I try to apply this experience to guiding Team riders in my role as chef d'équipe. I know that sports psychology is very popular today, but I confess to being skeptical of its place at the international level.

As chef d'équipe, I would not want to have to calm down a nervous rider and tell him or her not to worry. This may be appropriate at the in-gate of an adult/amateur jumper class, but if a rider has achieved enough to be on the Team, he or she should be able to overcome any nervousness and go in and perform well. I would rather tell a Team rider, even at his or her first Olympics, to go in the ring and get the job done.

Planning the strategy for the Team is the main job of the chef d'équipe. An important part of planning strategy is knowing the capabilities of the riders on the Team and determining when they should ride. Many chefs d'équipe, including myself, do not like to send the weakest horse-rider combination in first. The weakest, or least experienced rider usually benefits from seeing

A newcomer to grand prix ranks in 1991, Darlene Sandlin shows good form starting a turn in a jump-off. She has not stopped her horse Alley Oop in the air, but has indicated where she wants to go and is looking toward her next fence. (Photo © Cathrin Cammett)

Anne Kursinski and the stallion Starman are in perfect form over this spread jump at the Seoul Olympics. (Photo copyright © Tish Quirk)

the course ridden by another Team member. Seeing a stronger, more experienced person go in the ring and watching how this rider rides the course give the weakest rider confidence. Ideally, this rider will then think, "This course is not the monster I thought it was."

Besides showing the others how to ride the course, the first rider should come back and give his or her teammates feedback. Was a particular corner slippery? Did a line ride differently than expected when we walked the course? These observations are invaluable to the Team members still waiting to compete.

The concept of saving the best for last holds true for Team riding. At the end of the jumping order, I like to place the horse-

and-rider combination that is most likely to jump the course without faults. In my planning, I also consider this rider as the one who can, as they say, pull the fat out of the fire and put in a fast, clean jump-off round. This rider can win the competition, or, if your three previous scores have already won the class, you can save your best horse and rider to help the Team in the grand prix later in the show.

Although most riders who jump do not aspire to ride for the United States Equestrian Team, there are other opportunities to experience team riding, some of them at a pretty high level. Each year, the top four junior riders from each American Horse Show Association zone are chosen to represent their zone in the AHSA National Junior Jumper Championships at the Pennsylvania National Horse Show in Harrisburg, Pennsylvania. As in international competition, the riders compete on teams and individually. At the North American Young Riders' Championships, the top riders under the age of 21 in the United States, Canada, and Mexico compete head to head. There, riders in all three Olympic disciplines compete on teams and individually. Some horse shows offer competitions in which riders can choose their teams. Although these competitions are informal, they are fun and educational.

While not essential to the development of horse or rider, team competition is worthwhile for the additional experience it gives you and for the opportunity you gain to learn more about yourself and your horse. Even at the lower levels, riding on a team is yet another dimension of an ongoing learning experience.

I have been very lucky to have had the experience of representing the United States in several Olympic Games. I have also been very fortunate in my lifetime to ride a lot of good horses. I hope that what I have learned as a rider and a chef d'équipe for the Team and from the horses I have trained can further enhance the learning experiences of other riders.

8

Questions and answers

*W*ould you buy a horse that cribs or weaves?

Yes, if the horse can jump high and wide. There have been a lot of great horses that cribbed or weaved, including Untouchable, White Lightning, and Sharrar. The problem with horses that crib and weave is that it is hard to keep weight on them. A lot of Thoroughbreds, because of their excess energy, have these vices. However, if a horse is going to win the gold medal in the Olympic Games, I don't care if it cribs or weaves.

If Gem Twist were a stallion, do you think he would be as successful?

Although there is no way of truly knowing, my guess is that he would be just as good. His father, Good Twist, had a very good mind for his job. When jumping, he never thought of anything else. However, we were always careful not to combine showing and breeding. I would never consider having him cover a mare at a show, although I was asked many times. Good Twist, when being ridden or jumped, thought only about doing his job in the best way possible. Gem Twist is so much like his father that I can only believe he would have been the same way.

Is there anything I can feed my horse to make him jump higher?

Not that I know of. Of course, good nutrition is necessary for any horse to do well. A horse should have a properly balanced diet if it is to jump to its utmost potential. Some people feed their horses supplements to keep them healthy. Consult your veterinarian if you feel your horse is lacking any important nutrients and you think you may need to add a supplement to your horse's diet.

My horse sinks down when I get on him. Should I use more pads?

While more pads or a big sponge pad may help, your horse may have a problem that a veterinarian should examine. I do not want to prescribe thick pads as the answer for all horses that sink down when the rider gets on them. If the veterinarian says this is a normal condition for your horse, big cowboy pads or other types of thick pads may help. Also, try getting on the horse very lightly without quickly putting a lot of weight in the saddle.

My saddle slips back all the time, but I'm worried that a breastplate
will restrict my horse's movements. What do you think?

I have not found that a breast plate restricts a horse's movements or shortens its stride. There are many types of breast-
plates available. If you find the one you have restricts your
horse's movement, try a different style breastplate. I feel the
risk of restricting your horse's movement is minimal compared
to the problems you could have if the saddle slips back.

I see Gem Twist uses a figure-eight noseband. Should I use one too?

Not necessarily. Just because Gem Twist uses a piece of equipment does not mean you should as well. A figure-eight noseband keeps a horse from opening its mouth a lot. If your horse
does not have this problem, then you probably do not need this
type of noseband.

When would you use a shadow roll?

A shadow roll is a sheepskin noseband that fluffs up quite high.
It was popularized by driving and Standardbred trainers who
used it presumably to keep horses from shying at shadows on
the ground. As it restricts the horse's vision, a shadow roll will
often help a horse that spooks or shies a lot. It may also keep a
horse from putting its head up as it won't be able to see where
it is going.

My horse goes well in a wire snaffle, but it creates sores in his mouth.
What do you suggest?

A wire snaffle is an extreme bit for most horses and should be
used only if good riding skills do not work. If you are using a
double wire snaffle for its scissor effect, try wrapping latex tape
on the corners of the bit, which probably are causing the sores.
If your horse is prone to getting sores, don't use a wire snaffle
every day. Save it for the horse shows. Once your horse's
mouth gets sore the horse will, for sure, not perform at its best.

Anakonda with Frank Chapot at Hickstead, England in the mid-1960s, using a shadow-roll cavesson. This mare would spook a lot, especially at things on the ground, an odd-looking ground line on a jump, puddles, or even a dark-colored clump of grass. The shadow roll somewhat blocked her vision of these items and made her a lot easier to ride. (Copyright © Leslie Lane)

My horse leans on my hand and balances there. When I tried using a stronger bit he threw up his head. When I put draw reins on he tucked in his chin. What would you suggest I do?

Draw reins are fine if you don't constantly pull on them. They should be used to restrict a horse's head to the proper place, not pull the head into the chest. To get your horse soft and in proper balance you want to move your horse forward with your seat and leg. Stiffen your hand, but do not pull back. When you push your horse forward it will hit your hand and get soft. Essentially, you want to kick your horse forward to make it soft. Using very restrictive draw reins will teach a horse to lean on your hand. A constant pull on the horse's mouth is incorrect and does not solve the problem.

Which do you prefer to use—draw reins or a German martingale (draw reins that attach to a ring on the reins, rather than being held in the rider's hands)?

Draw reins, because you have the option of turning them loose or tightening them up. You have less control when you use a German martingale as you are limited to where they are fixed on the regular reins. A German martingale, however, is easier to use for someone inexperienced with regular draw reins. With a German martingale you only have to hold one rein in each hand and you don't have to worry about getting them too tight or too loose, as you do with draw reins.

I can't use a standing martingale in some classes, but my horse sticks his head in the sky when I take the martingale off. What should I do?

While a standing martingale is probably the best piece of equipment you can use to keep your horse's head down, when you can't use one you might try a running martingale (working your horse at home with draw reins). A running martingale will give you some leverage and act almost like draw reins. You might also try using a shadow roll. If a horse wearing a shadow roll tries to put its head up, the horse will not be able to see where it is going. Still, neither of these pieces of equipment is the perfect solution. You need to go back to your flatwork and work on getting your horse's head down. Then begin to mix flatwork with a little jumping so your horse will not feel a great difference when you go to jump in a competition.

I have been trying to teach my horse to do leg yields, turns on the haunches, and turns on the forehand, but my horse goes towards my leg instead of away from it. What should I do?

Sharper spurs will help some, but don't use it so much that your horse begins to kick back or buck. You also might try reinforcing your leg by touching the horse just behind the saddle with a whip. Some people teach a horse to move away from the rider's leg from the ground. They press against the horse's side and the rider's leg, forcing the horse to move when the rider's leg presses against the horse's side. I have not had much experience using this method, but I have seen it done successfully. With patience and persistence you should be able to teach your horse to move away from your leg.

My horse jumps over all the cavalletti rather than stepping through them. Is there a way to get him to go through them properly?

You will need a lot of patience to solve this problem. Start by walking your horse over a single cavalletti and turning at the same time to help the horse accept the cavalletti without jumping. Next, add a second cavalletti. Make sure you can walk through a pair of cavalletti before you attempt trotting through them. A lot of times you can get a horse to go through cavalletti better at a sitting trot, where you have more control, than at a posting trot. Many people start a young horse over too high a cavalletti, where the horse's natural instinct is to jump. I prefer to start a young horse over a rail or two-by-four on the ground. Once the horse gets used to stepping over these, I introduce the raised cavalletti.

My horse won't enter the ring. How can I get him through the in-gate?

Have an experienced person lead your horse into the ring while someone else follows behind with a whip of some kind. You don't want to chase the horse in as it may get excited and have a poor performance. If you are on your own, carry a long whip and try to trick him into going into the ring without getting the horse too upset.

My horse runs out the in-gate. What should I do?

Have a groom stand at the in-gate with a longe whip. First, however, experiment with a longe whip in some other place so when your horse sees a longe whip the horse will respect it and later be deterred from running out the in-gate. To prevent this problem from ever starting, never let your horse go directly out the in-gate after finishing a course. Always make at least one circle before leaving the ring.

How and when do you start a young horse over fences?

If you break your horse as a two-year-old, it should have some sort of discipline. Trotting a young horse over a rail on the ground or a crossrail is a nice way to introduce the horse to the canter and to leads without making it run faster. As it goes over a rail, a horse will often break into a canter. I prefer to use a chute to teach horses to jump as it is much easier for them to jump free than with a rider or on a longe line. There is no weight on their back or longe lines to get tangled in or pull on their mounts. The horses are perfectly free to adjust their stride and develop their eye without interference from a rider or trainer. I don't do any serious jumping with my young horses until they are at least three and sometimes four years old, depending on their development.

My horse bucks after every jump. How can I get him to stop doing this?

If your horse bucks after every jump there could be something physically wrong with the horse. Have a veterinarian examine the horse to make sure there is nothing wrong with its back that might make jumping painful. If your horse is just fresh, punish it so it knows when it jumps a fence it can't buck or run off. By punishing I do not mean you should hit the horse with a whip; this would probably only worsen the problem. Instead, after a jump do a half-halt or stop and back the horse so it knows that after it jumps it must come back and listen to your commands.

Two views of our jumping corral at home where we free school young horses over fences. A view of the empty corral. (Photo by Jackie Promaulayko)

A view of the corral with rails set to jump. (Photo by Jackie Promaulayko)

My horse has a problem making the distances. Is there anything I can do?

There is not much you can do to help a horse with a naturally short stride except possibly flatwork and extensions. Try to get your horse to lengthen its stride by pressing the horse forward without increasing speed. Just going faster will not make your horse's stride longer. Try some dressage-type work to make your horse come from behind. There is not much you can do to change Mother Nature. If your horse is naturally short-strided you may have to stay in classes where the jumps are small enough so that you can add extra strides.

My horse is sound. Should I give him Bute (Butozolitin) anyway?

No. Although I have never had this experience, some people believe Bute gives a horse a dead mouth. Some people with horses that must jog after each performance give their horses Bute "just in case." I think this is a waste. Like anything overdone, this is not good. Until the AHSA came up with rules for acceptable levels of Bute, a lot of horses were given amounts that were toxic or unnecessary. If there is no reason to give your horse Bute, then don't. It does not make horses jump higher or wider.

Do you think that if you are good "friends" with your horse, it will try harder when you ask?

There is a difference between being friends and letting your horse walk all over you. While it is great if you can have a good rapport with your horse, it must still remember who is boss. Some horses can be better "friends" than others. A horse that bites, kicks, and is generally ill-tempered will need more discipline and must learn to respect your commands if it is to perform at its best.

How do you feel about feeding a horse treats when it comes out of the ring?

This practice is popular in Europe. A lot of grooms give their horses a bite of grass, especially when they have been very good. I am not an advocate of giving treats, but if your horse has been especially good, you might give him a bit of grass or a pat on the neck after he performs. However, I would not advocate feeding a horse that sulks or runs out of the in-gate anything when the horse comes out. This can only make it want to come out the in-gate more.

My horse won't load. How can I get him to go on a trailer or van?

Back your trailer to the door of your barn or drop your ramp where you have a confined area and more or less a chute situation. Then lead the horse toward the trailer with a longe line or a very long leadshank so you can get out of the way in case the horse jumps into the truck or trailer. Basically, you want to get your horse in a confined situation where it can't avoid the ramp by going right or left. A person standing to the rear of the horse can urge him forward with a longe whip, but not too aggressively. You don't want the horse to jump in a way that would cause it to hurt itself. Once the horse is on the truck or trailer you may want to give it some feed or sugar and a pat on the neck. Make being inside a pleasant experience. Practice loading several times until your horse gets used to it.

If you are away from home and can't get your horse to load, try using two longe lines as wings. Many horses will go in easier once they realize they can not escape to the right or left. I once had a horse that would jump on the truck as soon as he saw the longe line come out.

My horse jumps out of the paddock. I hate not to let him be turned out at all. Is there anything I can try?

It is important for a horse to have free time in the paddock and not just be penned up in its stall except when it is ridden. The best solution is to find a paddock with a higher fence or one that is bigger in size. If this is not possible, you might try putting some hay in the center of the field to keep the horse's interest or turning the horse out with a paddock mate.

My horse jogs back to the barn. How can I stop it from doing this?

Many horses, especially Thoroughbreds and ex-racehorses, have a tendency to jog back to the barn. To avoid this problem, try taking different approaches back to the barn. You might also try turning your horse away from the barn as you return or taking a zig-zag route. Usually, jogging toward the barn is just a nervous habit, but it is a difficult problem to correct. Have patience. Try to understand what is causing the problem and experiment with ways to keep your horse relaxed.

What should I do if my horse has difficulty jumping wide oxers?

You are not going to solve the problem by jumping big, wide oxers. Start by jumping low oxers and then gradually spread the width. You can also begin by using two bamboo ground lines spread from the base of a vertical. Your horse can land on these without risking being hurt. After your horse jumps this fence easily, set up a small wide oxer. You might even fix a tight distance to it so you don't have to rush to it. You want to give your horse confidence to jump wide. When a careful horse is green it may jump too high trying not to hit the jumps. While you don't want to overjump your horse, you want to teach it to jump another dimension—width as well as height. Nevertheless, if your horse can't jump wide because it doesn't have the talent, you might want to consider getting a new horse.

What should I do if my horse is lame, but I'm close to being champion at a big show?

Leave your horse in the stall. If the horse is lame and you ride it, you may further injure its lame leg or put stress on its good leg, thus injuring it as well. It is never worthwhile to make a lame horse compete at the risk of hurting its career.

When I try to go fast in a jump-off, my horse runs off and won't turn. What can I do?

Proper flatwork is important in teaching your horse how to turn. Your horse must learn to do a turn on the haunches. The horse should respect your hand and rein. If you just pull your horse around a turn, you may lose its outside shoulder, allowing the horse to continue to drift to the outside of the turn. You must be able to make turns with your horse at the walk, trot, and canter before you try to work with jumps. If you are having trouble turning over jumps, go back to low jumps and even practice with a rail on the ground. I feel it is best to teach a horse to turn over low, easy jumps. If you try to teach your horse to turn over high fences, you may have to release so much over the top of the jump that you will have a hard time getting the horse back in control after the fence. You will also risk shaking the horse's confidence or having a wreck if the horse makes a mistake.

When should I turn inside a jump?

When it is faster. Usually turning inside is faster; however, what you do in the distance before the turn will make a difference as to which option is feasible and faster. If you leave out a stride to the fence before the turn you will land farther from that fence. In this case it may not be practical to take the inside route, as you will stop your horse so much to make the inside cut that it would have been faster to run around. If you take the normal number of strides or add a stride to the fence before the turn it will be easier to turn inside. Which option you choose will depend on how well your horse is trained and what it does best. If your horse turns well, then turning inside the jump is usually the faster choice.

My horse always stops at water jumps and liverpools. Is there a way I can get it to jump them?

Many people get into this problem by doing too much too fast. They try to jump a big liverpool that frightens the horse before having prepared it properly over smaller ones. There are all kinds of imitation liverpools on the market today made in a variety of materials, shapes, and sizes. Start with a narrow piece of blue canvas only a foot or two wide. You can also effect the look of a liverpool by using a dye in the water. Start off slow and narrow. Make the jump very inviting and use the rails for wings on the approach to make it difficult for your horse to run out. It is also a good idea to have people stand on each side of the liverpool to deter your horse from running right or left. Most horses can learn to jump water. It is rare to find one that will not jump water at all with proper and careful training.

A young horse starting to learn to jump a small artificial water jump. (Photo by Mary Chapot)

The horse progressing upwards over a more complex water jump. (Photo by Jackie Promaulayko)

Horse finally jumping a liverpool similar to the ones encountered at horse shows. (Photo by Jackie Promaulayko)

A larger artificial water jump with a rail in the center and a plastic rail on the landing to simulate the tape found at shows. The water is dyed. The water in this style jump should be set up no wider than 6 to 8 feet to start. (Photo by Jackie Promaulayko)

A very green horse over jumping the water. The rider, perhaps anticipating a stop, is a little bit behind the motion—not the worst place to be here. (Photo by Jackie Promaulayko)

The horse and rider more relaxed over a water jump with a rail in the center. (Photo by Jackie Promaulayko)

Finally, the water jump without a rail. The horse and rider are relaxed. This process can be done over a few days. (Photo by Jackie Promaulayko)

How would you ride to a puissance wall?

There are two thoughts to keep in mind when you jump a puissance wall. First, you want to jump the wall on a little bit of an angle. This not only makes it more difficult for the blocks to fall, but also gives you the option of closing the angle if you see the distance coming up long or opening the angle if the distance is coming up too short. Second, you want to get deep to the wall. You do not want to stand off too far from this tall jump.

I do not have a lot of money and can not afford to buy an expensive horse that would get me on the Team. Do I stand a chance of ever riding on the United States Equestrian Team?

Many people think of riding as an elitist sport only for the very wealthy. In reality, this is only true once in a while. The majority of riders come from modest backgrounds and have risen to the top by developing their skills. If you can ride well enough to win, the people who own the very expensive horses will get you to ride them. The Michael Matzs and Leslie Lenehans of the world were recognized as have very exceptional skills and are in demand to ride grand prix and Olympic prospects.

Glossary

ascending oxer A spread fence in which the top elements are not in the same horizontal plane, the front element being lower.

bell boots Protective boots for a horse's feet and coronary bands.

bone spur A spur-like bony growth occasionally observed on X rays. It is usually formed at the margin of joints or where ligaments attach to the bone.

bounce A gymnastic combination in which the horse jumps in over a jump, lands, and then immediately jumps out over another jump without taking a stride in between.

bowed tendon Thickening of the flexor tendons or their sheaths.

breastplate   A piece of equipment attached to the saddle to prevent it from slipping back on the horse.

brush jump   A type of jump with bush filler.

capped hock   A soft enlargement at the point of the hock, generally caused by kicking or rubbing.

cavalletti   For the purpose of this book, when I refer to cavalletti I am talking about 1 to 4 rails on the ground set 4 to 4-½ feet apart. They may also be mounted on a small base so they won't roll, but they should be no more than 6 to 8 inches high.

chef d'équipe   A team captain or coach of an equestrian team responsible for making arrangements for a national team both on and off the field.

conformation hunter   A hunter that is judged on its appearance as well as its performance.

contracted heels   A congenital or acquired condition where the posterior portion of the foot is narrow.

counter-canter   Cantering on the "off" or outside lead. The horse's head is bent to the outside and the rider must maintain an active leg to keep the horse from switching leads.

crossrail   Type of jump where the poles are set with one end in a cup and one end on the ground, forming an "X". This type of fence is most often seen as a starting jump for young horses or a warm-up jump in the schooling area.

curb   A firm enlargement at the back of the hock.

"daisy-cutter"   A way of describing a horse that moves very well, keeping a straight leg and skimming the ground.

double combination   Two fences set no more than 39' 5" apart that must be taken successively in one or two strides.

draw reins   A set of reins that run through the bit and attach to the girth either between the forelegs or under the skirt of the saddle.

dropped noseband   A noseband that fastens below the bit.

elevator bit   A type of bit that has an elongated shank and gives a rider more leverage.

figure-eight Exercise in which the horse describes a pattern done in the figure of an eight.

figure-eight noseband Noseband that fastens above and below the bit forming a figure eight with the center being high on the horse's nose.

flying change A change of lead done without breaking to the walk or trot.

free school Jumping a horse without a rider or the use of a longe line.

gag A type of bit in which rounded cheek pieces pass through holes at the top and bottom of the bit rings before attaching directly to the rein, so that when pressure is exerted the bit rises in the horse's mouth.

grob A sloping combination with a ditch at the bottom, requiring the horse to jump in, go down a slope, over the ditch, and up an incline over another fence.

groundline A rail or other decoration resting on the ground in front of a fence.

ground person An unmounted trainer or helper who can set jumps and may give directions.

hackamore A bitless bridle.

half-pirouette A half circle executed on two tracks with a radius the length of the horse. The horse's forehand moves around its haunches. Usually carried out at the collected walk or canter, the horse's head should be bent in the direction in which it is turning. Horse should maintain its impulsion and never move backwards or deviate sideways.

hand A degree of measurement used for measuring horses: 1 hand = 4 inches.

haunches-in A lateral exercise similar to the shoulder-in. As the horse moves forward the haunches are toward the inside and the horse is bent around the rider's inside leg.

hogsback A type of jump composed of three elements where the front and back elements are lower than the center one.

hunt meet A race meeting, usually held on one day, where the majority of the races are over fences.

hurdles   A type of low brush jump used in racing.

impulsion   A horse's power.

in-and-out   Two jumps set less than 39' 5" apart that can be taken in one or two strides.

lateral work   Movements where the horse moves sideways as well as forward.

leg yielding   A lateral movement where the horse moves away from the rider's leg. The horse's head is bent toward the rider's active leg and the horse moves in the opposite direction from which it is bent.

liverpool   A type of jump with water underneath.

longing   Training or exercising a horse by having it move on the end of a longe line in circles around the trainer. A trainer often uses a long whip to urge the horse on.

navicular disease   An often degenerative condition of a bone and its adjoining soft tissue structures encased by the foot.

Nations' Cup   A two-round international team competition where the best three out of four scores of each team count in each round.

offset   A bamboo pole that has been set in front of and slightly higher than a low vertical jump, creating a false groundline that is hard for the horse to judge.

oxer   A type of jump requiring the horse to jump width as well as height.

pelham   A bit with a shank and pieces for two reins that works on the bars of a horse's mouth as opposed to the cheeks.

plain snaffle   A mild type of bit with a smooth mouthpiece.

point-to-point   A type of informal race meeting.

poll   The top of the horse's head.

puissance class   Class that tests horse's ability to jump high.

refusal   Stopping at an obstacle that is to be jumped.

rein-back   To cause your horse to back up.

ring bone   Degenerative disease of the pastern joints, which in severe cases is characterized by a bony enlargement forming a ring around the front of the pastern.

rollback A prompt half turn at the canter. A rollback may be executed as an exercise on the flat similar to the half pirouette. It is often referred to as a tight turn back to a fence in a jump-off.

rolltop A solid type of jump with a curved top.

rub class A class in which faults are given for touching the top element of a jump as well as for knocking it down.

rubber bit A mild type of bit on which the mouthpiece is covered with rubber.

run-in shed A type of open shed in a field that gives a turned-out horse protection from the elements.

running martingale A type of martingale with rings through which the reins are run.

run-out Evading or passing the obstacle to be jumped.

scope A measure of a horse's ability to jump high and wide.

shelly hoof Refers to poor quality of hoof material that has a tendency to crack or flake.

shoulder-in A lateral movement. The horse moves forward with its body on an angle to the outside rail and its shoulders toward the center. The horse is bent around the rider's inside leg. When viewed from the front, the horse shows three tracks. The outside hind leg is on one track, the inside hind leg and outside front leg travel together on a second track, and the inside front leg moves forward on a third track.

sickle hock Excessive angulation of the hock.

sidebone A bony hardening of the lateral cartilage structures over the bulbs of the heels.

splint A bony enlargement of the fore or hind splint bones.

spread A jump consisting of more than one element requiring the horse to jump width as well as height.

square oxer An oxer where the front and back rails are the same height.

standing martingale A martingale that attaches directly from girth to noseband, restricting movement of the head.

steeplechasing A race held over fences.

straight-bar pelham   A type of bit that has a straight bar for a mouthpiece, as opposed to the jointed mouthpiece of the snaffle. This bit works on the bars of the horse's mouth rather than the cheeks.

studs   A removable type of heel for the horse's shoe, used on slippery surfaces for better traction.

Swedish oxer   A type of oxer in which the rails on the front element are slanted one way and the rail on the back element is slanted the other way. See pictures on pages 126 and 127.

timber fence   A type of fence made out of post and rail that horses race over.

triple bar   A type of jump composed of three elements of ascending heights.

triple combination   An in-and-out composed of three jumps.

turn on the forehand   A turn executed from a halt or walk where the horse's hind quarters move around its forelegs. The horse is bent to the inside and there should be no forward motion once the turn is started.

turn on the haunches   A turn executed from the walk where a horse's forehand moves around the hindquarters. The horse is bent around the rider's inside leg. In this exercise, the rhythm of the walk does not stop, nor should the horse take any steps backwards.

twisted snaffle   A type of snaffle bit where the mouthpiece is slightly twisted, giving it a rough surface, making it more severe than a plain snaffle.

twisted wire bit   A rather severe bit with a thin mouthpiece made from strands of metal twisted together.

two-track   A very difficult lateral movement where the horse moves sideways and forward at the same time. The horse's head is bent toward the direction it is traveling. The front part of the horse must always stay ahead of the hindquarters and care should be taken to maintain the same rhythm throughout. This exercise may be executed at the walk, trot, or canter.

under saddle class   A class on the hunter division where the horses are judged on their way of moving and do not jump.

vertical   A type of jump where all the elements are in the same vertical plane.

windpuff   A soft fluid-filled enlargement involving the joints, tendon sheaths, or bursae.

Index